Making MAGNIFICENT WOOD ART

Fox Chapel
PUBLISHING

Making MAGNIFICENT WOOD ART

CRAFTING IMAGINATIVE WORKS WITH EVERYDAY WOODWORKING TOOLS

Meleah Gabhart

© 2025 by Meleah Gabhart and Fox Chapel Publishing Company, Inc.

Making Magnificent Wood Art is an original work, first published in 2025 by Fox Chapel Publishing Company, Inc. The patterns contained herein are copyrighted by the author. Readers may make copies of these patterns for personal use. The patterns themselves, however, are not to be duplicated for resale or distribution under any circumstances. Any such copying is a violation of copyright law.

ISBN 978-1-4971-0554-6

Library of Congress Control Number: 2025940111

Shutterstock used: marukopum (abstract design, used throughout); Renee Foskett (ambrosia maple, 20); Vladimir Wrangel (aspen, 20); Tony Savino (bloodwood, 20); MARGRIT HIRSH (canarywood, 20); Taro_since2017 (cypress, 20); Formatoriginal (eucalyptus, 20); Labraaten (heart pine, 20); Svetliy (sapele, 21); h.yegho (tigerwood, 21); Maksym Bondarchuk (wenge, 21); SimoneN (zebrawood, 21); Rawpixel.com (Seurat painting, 26); Jason Patrick Ross (Mount Rushmore, 49); Paolo Grandi (marble relief, 49).

To learn more about the other great books from Fox Chapel Publishing, or to find a retailer near you, call toll-free at 800-457-9112 or visit us at *www.FoxChapelPublishing.com*. We are always looking for talented authors.
To submit an idea, please send a brief inquiry to acquisitions@foxchapelpublishing.com.
Or write to:
Fox Chapel Publishing
903 Square Street
Mount Joy, PA 17552

Printed in China
First printing

Because working with woodworking tools and other materials inherently includes the risk of injury and damage, this book cannot guarantee that creating the projects in this book is safe for everyone. For this reason, this book is sold without warranties or guarantees of any kind, expressed or implied, and the publisher and the author disclaim any liability for any injuries, losses, or damages caused in any way by the content of this book or the reader's use of the tools needed to complete the projects presented here. The publisher and the author urge all readers to thoroughly review each project and to understand the use of all tools before beginning any project.

Introduction to Making Wood Art

When making the sculpted wood mosaics in this book, each person's wood art, whether an aspen forest or a mandala, will bear their own artistic stamp. No two pieces will look the same.

I most often call what I do "sculpted wood mosaics." When you envision a mosaic, maybe you see an arrangement of very small pieces of tile or material. The tile pieces are about the same size and randomly shaped. I think this definition is the traditional way to view mosaic art. But what happens if the mosaic pieces are not random and have intentional shapes that help portray the subject of the art? Suddenly, you have introduced a whole new dimension, a whole new breadth to the work. This new dimension is what distinguishes sculpted wood mosaics from traditional mosaics.

In this book, I'll walk you through making your own wood art step by step, from finding a subject and building a pattern to sculpting and putting together the individual pieces. I'll share the many moments in the process where creative decisions shape the final piece. I'll guide you through how I make those choices using examples and how you can develop your own creative intuition to bring your vision to life.

Every step of these projects is an opportunity for you to put aside following the rules and lean into your intuition. By following these steps and becoming familiar and adept with the techniques, you'll be able to understand the entire process so that you can know when to break the rules and make up your own, intelligently and creatively.

When making the sculpted wood mosaics in this book, each person's wood art, whether the iconic Frida Kahlo or a subject from nature, will bear their own artistic stamp. No two pieces will look the same.

When I disappear into my workshop for a week or two and emerge with a work of art, even iconic images such as Frida Kahlo or the Afghan Girl, they have a stamp of my unique perspective and view of the world. I would wager that two people, following the same directions for a project in this book, would end up with two unique mosaics that are not exactly like my finished project. In those differences, you can probably find your own stamp, and my hope is to start you on the path to your own artistic journey.

Forever in creation,
Meleah

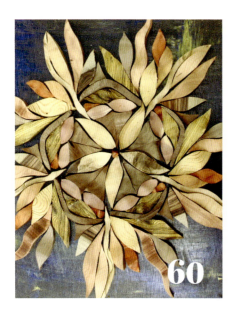

 112

 121

Contents

Chapter 1: Tools and Materials **8**
    Tools 10
    Wood Selection 15

Chapter 2: Pattern Creation **24**
    Visualizing Your Image as a Mosaic 26
    Essential Elements in Your Pattern 27
    Methods for Drawing a Pattern 33
    Tips for Refining Your Pattern 36

Chapter 3: Techniques **40**
    Making a Backer Board 42
    Preparing the Pattern 43
    Sculpting the Wood 45

Chapter 4: Projects **58**
    Floral Mandala Mosaic 60
    Rose Reverie Mosaic 66
    Carved Canopy Mosaic 72
    Yellow Wood Mosaic 84
    Patterns 95

Chapter 5: Journey of a Wood Artist **99**

Index **128**

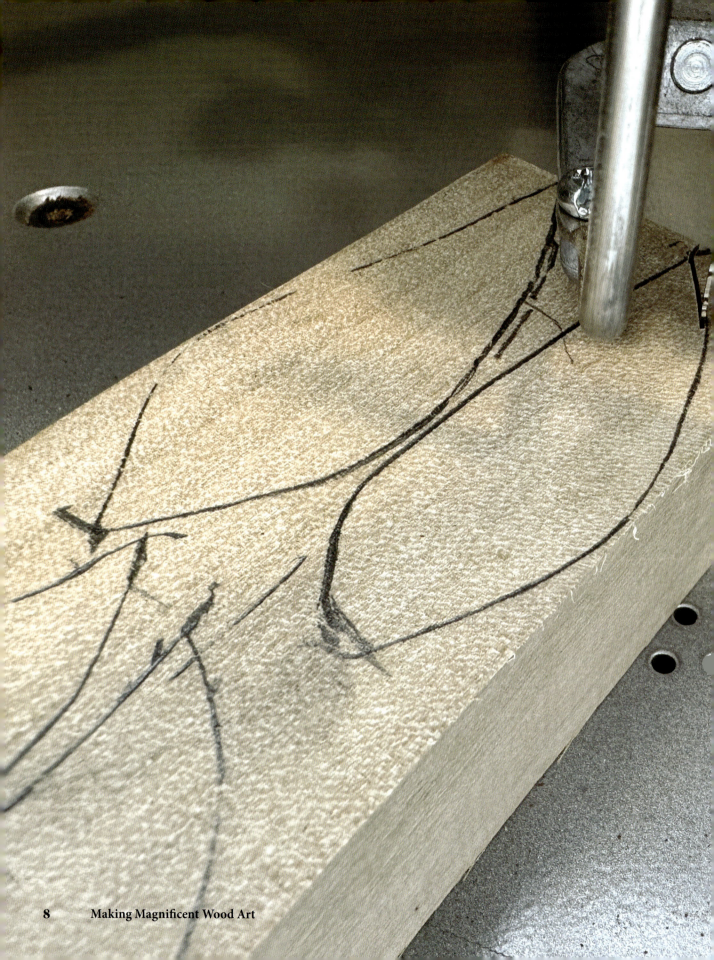

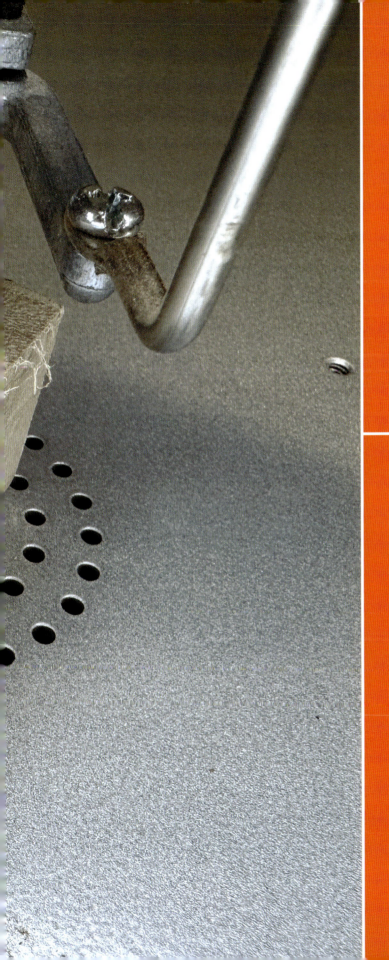

Chapter 1: Tools and Materials

Whether you have a fancy wood shop or are working from a dusty corner of your garage, let's take a look at the equipment and materials you need to get started. About 10 years ago, I started out with a jigsaw and a little bitty belt sander, so strictly speaking, while some things are not absolutely necessary, they are incredibly convenient.

My dusty little projector is perfect for projecting images from my phone onto the hardboard.

Tools

Patternmaking Tools

Camera—Take photos of your image. A high-res phone camera works just as well, and you can potentially use the photo-editing options on your phone.

Photo-Editing Software or Application—Applications that convert a photograph or image into a sketch should offer a detailed line drawing, rather than just an outline of the objects within the photo. By using several different applications, such as Sketchify, Canva, BeFunky, or ChatGPT, you can gather a lot of line-drawing information to help make a pattern from your image.

Pencil and Permanent Marker—Use a sharpened 2B graphite pencil or fine-tipped black Sharpie for tracing the pattern pieces onto the wood. For darker wood or highly striped wood, the fine-tipped marker can be easier to see when you are cutting.

Paper—You can purchase a roll of white project paper from a local craft store or online. I usually get the 30" (76.2cm) roll, which works for most projects. If my project dimensions are greater than 30" (76.2cm), I tape two pieces together to get the desired dimensions.

Projector—I use the DBPower mini projector. It is inexpensive, compact, and easy to set up with Bluetooth to connect your phone or camera.

Scissors—Don't forget the basics! A good pair of scissors will serve you for a long time. Just make sure you are only cutting paper to maintain a clean cut.

Tape Measure—Retractable tape measures are great. I recommend getting one that goes up to at least 10' (3m), though you won't need that much when working on the mosaics featured in this book.

Hardboard—This backing material is found at home-improvement stores in panels or sheets. You can have the store cut this to your size specifications or cut it yourself with a jigsaw.

Spray Adhesive—Spraying a large area on your hardboard is much easier than painting it on, and it is less likely to dry up by the time you start attaching materials. Make sure you buy one that is meant for wood.

Safety Equipment

Ear Protection—I have very sensitive ears, so I wear hearing-protector earmuffs when operating any saws or sanders. Ear plugs work but not as well.

Eye Protection—Wear clear safety glasses at all times so you do not forget to put them back on as you go back and forth to your scroll saw and band saw. If you wear prescription glasses, these will protect you as long as they cover your eyes generously and fit closely.

Finger Protection—When sanding, I wear silicone fingertip protectors to prevent sanding off the skin of the fingertips. Better safe than sorry.

Normally I protect my fingers from sanders with fingertip protectors, but sometimes going back and forth from saw to sander, the cut prevention gloves stay on. Be especially careful when wearing gloves near an oscillating sander, as it may grab a loose glove and wrap it up fast!

Gloves—Let me be clear: there are no gloves that completely protect your fingers and hands from saw blades. Keeping your fingers and hands away from saw blades are what prevent cuts. However, as a small protection when cutting out or sculpting small pieces, I wear cut-resistant kitchen gloves because they offer some protection, and they are thin enough so I can still feel the wood.

Backer Board

I have found ½" (1.3cm) thick, sanded plywood to be the most reliable backer board material. It is easy to paint, easy to cut, and easy to adhere the mosaic wood to it. However, wood boards have to be glued together and biscuited, and they will still show seams. Please note this applies only to the wood used as backer board—I discuss the requirements for wood used as mosaics in the section Wood Selection (page 15).

For backing, I have used raw steel before, but a metal shop has to cut it, the steel has to be cleaned free of oils, and then it must be scored with a metal grinder on the areas where the mosaic will be glued down for optimal adherence. Other surfaces, like glass or tile, would need some surface texture for optimal adherence of the mosaic wood pieces, although I have not used these materials.

Cutting & Adhering Tools

Bandsaw with ⅛" (3.2mm) Blade, 10–14 TPI—I love a band saw when I am cutting thick wood, making longer cuts, and making straighter cuts, although this blade size will make some pretty tight turns. The

There sits my beast of a bandsaw. Adjust her properly everyday and she will pay you dividends in smooth(ish) and easy cuts.

Chapter 1: Tools and Materials

bandsaw is a badass machine, but with this type of saw, you only get what you pay for. I have to warn you: bandsaws are finicky and must be adjusted daily as well as after a blade change. The upper and lower guides around the blade **must** be kept adjusted because an unguided blade can spring back and is very, very dangerous. Plus, you can get a lot of chatter in an unguided, too tight, or too loose blade, leading to really rough cuts. I have learned the hard way to take time each day to fine-tune my beautiful bandsaw, a Laguna 14|12.

This Grizzly table saw is the little saw that could. While it is a bit on the small side for cutting a whole sheet of plywood, with two people, it works out. It also cuts all of my wood frames.

There are no excuses for not cutting on the angle when you have a table tilt feature on your scroll saw.

Table Saw—You do not need to buy a table saw if you do not already have one. Cutting the backer board evenly and square requires a table saw, but many home-improvement stores will cut this for you. I have a nice table saw but often just have the store cut the sheet of plywood to my specifications so I can fit it in my SUV. Another optional use for the table saw is making a frame for your sculptural mosaic.

Scroll Saw with Universal Blades #3, #5, and #7, 10–15 TPI—A scroll saw is a very specific saw that is made to cut thinner wood and cut tight turns. I can cut up to 2" (5.1cm) thick wood on my scroll saw, but I have to take it really slow and not push the wood into the blade, as well as **allow** the blade to cut its way through the wood. A lesson in patience for sure. I can use my scroll saw for all the projects in this book and have no problems. Plus, the scroll saw is a less-aggressive saw than the bandsaw, and I like to use it especially when the wood pieces are quite small or I am cutting at an angle. These cuts require your hands to be close to the saw blade. My scroll saw (a Grizzly G0969) can cut these angles by tilting the table, but I often forget I have this feature and cut by holding the wood piece at an angle.

Quite by accident, I discovered that I like foil tape over blue painter's tape in the shop. After borrowing my husband's, the foil tape worked so well that I bought my own roll.

Tape—When I use tape in my work, I usually use foil tape because it can make a strong bond to the wood. Other tape may work just as well, but this is my preference. Applying a strip of tape on the backer board where you will be cutting it on the table saw helps to prevent splintering from the blade.

Microfiber Cloth—Keep your workspace clean with a good cloth. In my experience, microfiber will adhere better to sawdust than other types of cloths.

Needle-Nose Pliers—Often when gluing down the mosaic, picking up the small pieces with your fingers can shift other adjoining pieces. I use needle-nose pliers to be more precise.

Glue—This is used for gluing the mosaic pieces to the backer board. I have found that Gorilla Max Strength Construction Adhesive Clear in a tube yields the best adherence, is viscous enough to not spread too much, and dries slightly flexible. This slight flexibility can prevent the glue from cracking in case the final piece is dropped or mishandled. My second choice is a viscous CA glue. The advantage of this glue is its drying time and viscosity. When gluing down pieces of mosaic that are partially entwined, it helps to have fast-drying glue so each piece can fully set before gluing the adjacent one down to prevent accidentally moving them out of place.

Sanding Equipment

Sanding Mop—A sanding mop is a wonderful addition to your sanding repertoire. I wish I had known about a sanding mop earlier, then I would have saved my fingers and the drudgery of finishing sanding. The mops need something to spin them, and I attach them to an electric drill with a foot pedal. The best option is to attach them to a drill press because it maintains a set speed and you can focus on just sanding.

Oscillating Drum Sander with ½", ¾", and/or 1" (13, 19, and 25mm) **Drums, 180 and 240 Grit**—The drum

For my mop sander, I attach a foot pedal to the drill so I have both hands free. You could also hold the drill in a vice attached to your work table.

I cannot imagine sanding without this tool. The oscillating drum on top moves up and down and sands difficult-to-access areas on the wood.

sander is great for sanding curved wood pieces. Every project has curved pieces, and the more dramatic the curves (shorter, deeper), the smaller the drum needed to fit into those curves. I find that a ½" (13mm) and 1" (25mm) drum can handle about everything I throw at them. Longer curved pieces like the trunk pieces of the tree project would benefit from a drum that is at least 1" (25mm) or larger. However, I have successfully sanded them with the smallest drum as well. If you absolutely do not have a way to get a drum sander, use a Dremel with a barrel sander attached. It will do the trick, just a bit slower.

Finishing Tools & Materials

Paintbrush—I use a 2" (5.1cm) or small roller for painting the backer board.

Gloves—Latex, disposable gloves are good for applying paint and acrylic finish at the end.

This product, after drying, leaves the wood exactly the same tone and color.

Acrylic Finish—Used for preserving wood color from UV. I use clear, acrylic, non-yellowing, exterior matte finish varnish from Modern Masters. I find it to be the best at soaking into the wood and preserving color. Apply two coats for full coverage.

The belt sander works best for sanding areas with minimal inside curvature. It's great for sanding away excess wood material.

Small Belt Sander, 180 and 240 Grit—This is the little sander that can do almost anything. This sander is best used for sides, tops, and bottoms of longer pieces that have gradual curves.

This metallic paint creates an ethereal feeling rather than the solid, flat look of acrylic paint.

Paint—Use either a thin paint wash (diluted acrylic paint) for wood, an acrylic transparent wood stain, or metallic paints from Modern Masters (which are transparent, real metallic finishes). Regular undiluted-acrylic, latex, or oil paint creates a solid layer between the backer board and the wood mosaic pieces and prevents the wood mosaic pieces from adhering directly to the backer board. I paint my backer boards with complementary colors—such as blues, greens, silvers, violet, and black—so that the mosaic pieces stand out.

14 Making Magnificent Wood Art

Finishing Options

Your mosaic project is mounted on a ½" (1.3cm) plywood backer board and the edges are not finished. What to do? I suggest three options here, though these are just ideas to get your creative juices flowing.

From the gallery of my work (starting on page 108), you can see that most of my art is framed. I do not make my own frames—and that is by design. I am not a carpenter. Measuring, angles, and exacting precision have never been my strengths, nor are they the rhythm I work best in. My creative process requires flexibility, intuition, and an openness to the unexpected that I find in each piece of wood. Framing, by contrast, demands control and structure—qualities essential to a beautiful, well-built frame but foreign to the way I work.

Earlier in my career with some of my more complex pieces, I would design a thoughtful and artistic frame and then have a master carpenter friend make it, believing that the frame must also be art. In more recent years, I have felt, although these natural wood frames are beautiful, they actually divert viewer focus away from the mosaic art. Now my husband makes me simple, sturdy frames using hardwood like maple or ash, and I paint them—usually with the Modern Masters metallic paint so they blend with the backboard.

One recent exception to this minimalist frame epiphany is my Frida Kahlo mosaic. I hired my carpenter friend to build a large, curved frame we both designed, which he crafted from sapele. I was thinking that her bold, colorful style needed a maximalist frame, something more in keeping with her vibe. While it works well and is beautiful, if I had to do it over, I would not have made her an exception; I would have kept the frame unobtrusive and minimal and let her magnificence fully shine. It comes down to a matter of taste.

Leave the sides bare. You might prefer a clean look that does not distract from the mosaic art and does not require any framing expertise. In this case, I recommend sanding the sides and painting them with the same color as the backer board. Attach a simple picture-hanging hardware on the back, which can be purchased at craft and home-improvement stores; just make sure you buy one that can hold the right weight.

Simple painted frame. This is my go-to, since it provides an outline or a viewpoint and keeps the focus on the art. I recommend using solid wood because, if you have worked this hard on your mosaic, you honor it with a solid, real-wood frame. Most of these pieces are made at nonstandard sizes, so you may not find the correct frame in stores. You can make a frame yourself, which allows you to finish it how you wish: paint, stain, or raw wood. However, a framing professional can work with you on making exactly what you want while providing experienced advice.

Artistic frame. For a few of my art pieces, I designed a live edge on one side of my frames (the horse mosaic, *Bo*, and the tree, *Sway*) that give them a feeling of movement and appear to continue the piece outside the frame. You could do this yourself, make a curved frame, make the bottom frame edge thicker, or invent another option. However, I do recommend keeping it simple.

Wood Selection

In almost all my mosaics, I use wood to illustrate soft things like birds, animals, and humans. Funny enough, hardwoods do that best, as you will read later on. In fact, one of the things I love the most about using wood is this paradox. I often overhear people in my show space wondering what material I use because they cannot fathom it is wood.

Not forcing the wood to be what we want it to be allows the wood to be part of the decision-making. It can be coaxed by choosing wood whose grain or imperfections inspire a pattern or by choosing salvaged wood whose size and shape restrictions can inspire its use. This more spontaneous approach really gives the mosaic an organic and alive feeling rather than a rigid or overdesigned feeling. With that in mind, you can have a more intimate relationship with your wood as you work with it.

When choosing wood for your sculptural mosaics, the four primary considerations are thickness, grain, hardness, and color.

Thickness of Wood

Nearly all mosaic projects are enhanced by creating depth with multiple wood thickness. Creating depth can be as simple as using thicker wood for objects in the foreground (closest to the viewer) and thinner wood for objects in the middle ground and background (farther and farthest away). While these may have a very slight difference in thickness, even just ½" to 1" (1.3 to 2.5cm), it is enough to create a strong illusion of depth.

Determining what thickness you want your wood boards to be depends on what you are trying to achieve. If you want a chunkier, more tactile sculpture, then use 1" (2.5cm) thick boards and up to 2" (5.1cm). Because almost every sculpture has areas of thicker wood and areas of thinner wood, I usually do not use boards less than ½" (1.3cm) thick for the thinner areas to allow at least ½" (1.3cm) of depth for the sculpting cuts. Deeper carvings create an overall sense of motion and have a big tactile presence that allows for making deep sculpting cuts. I also rarely exceed 2" (5.1cm) for the thicker areas because the wood becomes much more difficult to cut and sculpt.

In both of these examples, I used wood that was a full 2" (5.1cm) thick in the highest areas. This allowed me a deeper sculpting cut (see the wing feathers) and a greater rounding effect of the tree trunk.

Use of wood thickness for creating depth can be as simple as using thicker wood for the foreground and thinner wood for the background. While these two areas may be only ½" (1.3cm) or less difference in thickness, it is enough to create a strong illusion of depth.

Grain and Variations

Examine your wood for some interesting grain patterns in the board, such as swirls, waves, and structurally sound knots. (To make sure the knots are structurally sound, check for any dry rot or powdery wood that could indicate a compromised knot. Gently tap the knot with a hammer, and if there is no "give" or movement, the knot is likely

I took advantage of the wood thickness to cut deep sculpting curves here. They create incredible ripples throughout the birds body, giving it an overwhelming sense of motion in flight.

For repetitive pieces, such as leaves, petals, and hair, make sure the grain direction runs the same way in each of the pieces.

This is an example of allowing the grain to inform your pattern. I love old growth cedar, and this knot gave me the perfect focal point for a tree trunk. This is how the Carved Canopy project (page 72) began.

sound.) Often, where you have these interesting grain patterns in a board, the wood is darker than the rest of the board. Choosing wood with these tonal variations can help to create texture and depth in your mosaic.

While you're choosing wood and reviewing the grain, you'll also want to refer to the pattern you've chosen for your mosaic (see page 95). Choosing interesting wood is one thing, but knowing where and how grain fits into the mosaic is another entirely. In creating your pattern, you'll have laid the foundation for how the mosaic will look and much of the artistic process lies in these decisions. Here are some general points to remember. They are not rules but rather suggestions for grain decisions within your mosaic. Always experiment, and your eye will catch what works and what does not.

Be aware of repeated pieces in your mosaic, such as leaves. For these pieces, position the grain in a consistent direction. For instance, for leaves in a tree, the grain would run from stem to tip for all

For small mosaic pieces, use finer-grained wood with less grain contrast.

Chapter 1: Tools and Materials

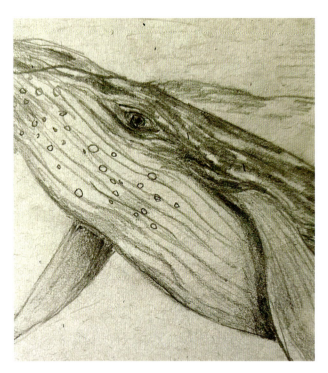

the leaves. For flower petals, the grain runs from left to right, and for strands of hair, the grain follows the flow of the hair, from top to bottom. Whatever you decide, be consistent for repeating pieces. One exception is when the grain waves or swirls, in which case you can use any direction you like.

Use less distinct grain for smaller pieces. When mosaic pieces are small and not part of a strongly directional pattern, then grain direction is not as important. Use smooth, finer-grained wood that naturally has less grain contrast. This will allow you to cut the pattern pieces from any direction of the grain.

Use sketches to help determine grain direction. Most often, sketching is a reliable source of information on how the grain direction should run within the mosaic. Sketches are made up of lines that reveal the subject's construction that may be difficult to

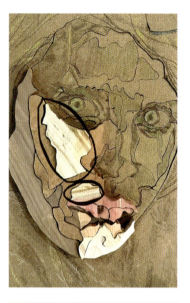

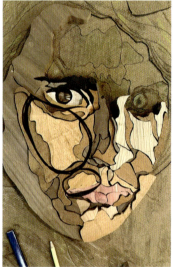

When making of the Afghan Girl, I used a bold linear-grained wood for the cheek and upper lip (circled). I thought it would give the face some strong direction and structure. Instead, the grain lines disrupted the continuity between the facial pieces, and I replaced it with a smooth cherry.

A sketch of your subject, a whale in this case, gives important information about grain direction. Notice how I mimicked the striations in the sketch when I chose wood for the whale pieces.

18   Making Magnificent Wood Art

see from a photo. Find a sketch someone has done of your subject or sketch it yourself. The direction of your sketch lines will usually tell you the direction best suited for your wood grain. For example, if you are sketching a tree trunk, your pencil will go up and down the tree, not left to right. This guideline nearly always works.

Take overhead photos of your mosaic to identify grain misfits. I like to take overhead photos about every hour and review them to make artistic decisions. As you fill in your pattern with wood, you may find a particular piece that stands out (see the Afghan Girl). Experiment with changing the grain direction of the wood piece and see if that makes the overall mosaic better. You may find that it's the shape of that particular pattern piece that doesn't work, and you need to redesign that part of the pattern. Or perhaps the color of the wood you chose for that area looks out of place. By studying your overhead photo, I feel confident you will better understand what changes need to be made. If you are still at a loss, make one of the changes I just mentioned, and in your next overhead photo, you will see immediately what is off and know what to do next.

Wood Hardness

Hardwoods are the best types of wood to use for sculptural mosaics. Hardwoods tend to be hard with tight grains that are less likely to break with sculpting. This quality also allows for a smoother finish. Softwoods, such as pine, poplar, spruce, and cypress, are more delicate, not very remarkable in color or grain, and not always suitable for sculpting into small pieces. Because of their softness and looser grain, they tend to break easily. One exception is eastern red cedar, which has a spectacular color and can be fairly dense toward the center. In the chart on the following pages, I've included information for your reference on many of the woods I use.

Strongly striped grains, such as tigerwood, zebrawood, and some canarywood, are ultimately difficult to place within a mosaic because most projects have natural curved lines that the linear stripes cannot follow well. However, in some instances where mosaic pieces are long and linear, strongly striped hardwoods could be incorporated with great interest.

Consult the table on the following pages for the best wood for your project.

Color variations within boards and between species can beautifully mimic tonal differences in nature, as you would find among the leaves of trees. I used walnut, maple, heart pine, poplar, yellowheart, and padauk.

Chapter 1: Tools and Materials **19**

Useful Woods for Making Mosaics

Photo	Name of Wood	Color	Notes on Workability	Grain Pattern
	AMBROSIA (WORMY) MAPLE	Whitish-gray or red; dark markings.	Moderately easy to work with but may burn with high speed tools.	Unusual markings from insect decay. Low visible grain pattern.
	AMERICAN BLACK WALNUT	Light to dark brown.	Easy to work when the grain is regular and straight.	Medium visible grain.
	ASH	Light to medium brown.	Moderately difficult to work with. May dull saw blades. Moderately easy to sand.	Irregular grain pattern.
	ASPEN	Pale cream to light brown.	Easy to work with, but because of interlocking grain, may not sand to a polish.	Medium visible grain pattern. Usually straight grain.
	BLOODWOOD	Bright to brownish red.	Difficult to work with. Use sparingly since it can be difficult to sculpt, will dull or break your blades, burns easily when cut or sanded, and is extremely tough to sand down.	Low visible grain pattern.
	CANARYWOOD	Yellow-orange with dark streaks.	Easy to work with and sand.	Highly visible linear grain lines. More difficult to place within a mosaic.
	CHERRY	Light pinkish to golden brown.	Easy to work with and sands to a polish.	Low visible grain pattern. Not always linear.
	CYPRESS	Golden to light brown.	Easy to work with and sand.	Medium visible grain pattern. Usually straight-grained.
	EASTERN RED CEDAR	Red, dark pink, red brown.	Very easy to cut and sand.	Low visible grain pattern. Knots can be unstable.
	EBONY	Black.	Difficult to work with. Use sparingly since it can be difficult to sculpt, will dull or break your blades, burns easily when cut or sanded, and is extremely tough to sand down.	Low visible grain pattern.
	EUCALYPTUS	Light brown to darker red.	Very easy to cut and sands easily.	Medium visible grain pattern. Some interlocking.
	GUM	Whitish to gray-red.	Easy to work with and sands to a fine polish.	Low visible grain pattern. Not always linear.
	HARD MAPLE	White or cream to reddish hue.	Moderately easy to work with but will burn with high-speed tools. Denser than soft maple.	Low visible grain pattern.
	HEART (HEARTWOOD) PINE	Golden to reddish brown.	Easy to work with and sands to a fine polish.	Medium visible grain pattern.
	HICKORY	Light to medium brown.	Difficult to work with. Use sparingly since it can be difficult to sculpt, will dull or break your blades, burns easily when cut or sanded, and is extremely tough to sand down.	Medium visible grain pattern.

Useful Woods for Making Mosaics

Photo	Name of Wood	Color	Notes on Workability	Grain Pattern
	HOLLY	Pale buttery color; uniform color.	Moderately easy to work, except for numerous knots.	Barely visible grain pattern. Good for areas needing a bright white.
	MAHOGANY	Golden browns to dark reds.	Very easy to cut and sands easily.	Low visible grain pattern.
	OSAGE ORANGE	Bright yellow to brown (oxidized).	Easy to work with and sands to a fine polish.	Medium visible grain pattern. Usually straight-grained.
	PADAUK	Bright orange to dull red.	Easy to work with and sand.	Medium visible grain pattern. Usually straight-grained.
	PINK IVORY	Pale, dark, or vibrant pink.	Moderately difficult to work with. May dull saw blades and burn when sanding.	Low visible grain pattern.
	POPLAR	Green to light brown.	Easy to work with and sands to a fine polish.	Low visible grain pattern.
	PURPLEHEART	Dark to brownish purple.	Difficult to work with. Use sparingly since it can be difficult to sculpt, will dull or break your blades, burns easily when cut or sanded, and is extremely tough to sand down.	Medium visible grain pattern. Usually straight-grained.
	ROSEWOOD	Golden brown to dark red-brown.	Moderately difficult to work with. May dull saw blades and burn when sanding.	Medium visible grain pattern. Usually straight-grained.
	SAPELE	Golden to dark reddish-brown.	Moderately easy to work with. May dull saw blades and burn when sanding. Finishes to a polish.	Medium visible grain pattern. Usually straight-grained.
	SYCAMORE	Bright white to darker tan.	Very easy to cut. Because of the interlocking grain, it does not sand to a polish.	Barely visible grain pattern.
	TIGERWOOD	Reddish-brown with dark streaks.	Moderately difficult to work with. May dull saw blades and burn when sanding.	Highly visible linear grain lines. Dark striations. More difficult to place within a mosaic.
	WENGE	Dark brown to black.	Difficult to work with. Use sparingly since it can be difficult to sculpt, will dull or break your blades, burns easily when cut or sanded, and is extremely tough to sand down.	Highly visible linear grain lines. Dark striations. More difficult to place within a mosaic.
	YELLOWHEART	Golden to pale yellow.	Easy to work with. The grain is regular and straight.	Medium visible grain pattern.
	ZEBRAWOOD	Light brown with dark streaks.	Moderately easy to work with. Cuts well but may not sand to a polish because of interlocking grain.	Highly visible linear grain lines. More difficult to place within a mosaic.

Chapter 1: Tools and Materials

Wood Color and Combinations

I almost exclusively use natural wood colors in all my mosaics. There are several ways you can use wood color to enhance the look of your sculpted mosaics.

Use different colors within the same board or different species to create tonal differences in your mosaic. Color variation is everywhere. A tree full of leaves does not have one shade of green but hundreds. These hundreds of different tones are created by light hitting the leaves at different angles. There are color variations on your own face: your lips are red, your skin is a solid color, your eyebrows and eyelashes are a color, and your eyes are white with an iris color. More subtly, your jawline casts a dark shadow on your neck, your cheekbones cast a shadow on your jaw that gives your face contour, your orbital arch casts a shadow on your eyes, and the list goes on.

If the color variation you want to portray is more random, like the leaves of a tree, you can use several ways to represent this phenomenon in your mosaic. The easiest way to capture this phenomenon in your mosaic is to use wood that has darker and lighter

The sides of Frida's face and most of her neck are in shadow (I used a bit darker wood), while the front forehead, nose, and chin are lit up. Early on, I decided where the light was coming from (directly overhead), placing the shadowed areas to create that effect.

The upper photo really captures the idea of the sun shining from the top right, where I used maple for the leaves. Gradually, the tree leaves darken as you move away from the right side; especially inside the canopy, the leaves darken to a walnut. The lower photo is an example of using a fairly monochromatic color scheme, but the wood itself has variation within.

areas within the same board. That area of your mosaic will not feel like a solid, flat color but will reflect the idea of natural color tones.

Another option is using two or more different wood species that have a very similar color. Such combinations could be two different mahoganies, ash and gum, and yellowheart and Osage orange, for example. By combining different wood species that have similar colors, your mosaic can suggest the multiple color values in nature.

Use different colors for shading. You may want to create the illusion of shading or shadows in your project. For instance, a tree trunk may have a shaded side and a sunny side. For mosaic pieces on the shaded side, you could use darker-toned wood, such as walnut, and on the sunny side, lighter tones, such as maple. With even more precision, shading on a face—such as Frida Kahlo's—helps to define the contours and gives the illusion of prominence (her jawline) and recessed areas (the sides of her nose and neck).

Use different wood species for different colors within your mosaic. In addition to representing the many shades and tones created by light, your mosaic pieces can represent the true colors of your subject. For example, the leaves of a tree in the autumn months have yellows, reds, purples, and browns. Choosing wood with these colors can enliven the mosaic with a more realistic look. On the other hand, choosing a nice variety of blacks, browns, and white/light tones for the leaves can have the dramatic effect of a black-and-white photograph.

Let your imagination go in terms of the colors, allowing the shape of the pieces to create the subject. Finally, you can choose whatever wood colors you wish for your mosaic. Let the shapes themselves create the resemblance to your subject, while your colors can be wild and fun.

This is an example of not using true-to-life colors but allowing the overall shape of the pieces to represent the heron. I used bright pink cedar and dark walnut for the feathers, resulting in a stunning contrast that somehow works.

Chapter 1: Tools and Materials

Chapter 2: Pattern Creation

Now that you understand what tools, materials, and woods are generally needed, you'll need to choose or create the pattern. Pattern creation or choices are not about locking things in—it's about sketching a flexible map. The choices you make here will inform your materials and guide your sculpting, but they're meant to evolve as your relationship with the piece deepens.

In this wolf portrait, notice how small, sculpted shapes of wood come together to make a whole image—similar to Seurat's pointillism.

Seascape at Port-en-Bessin, Normandy. Seurat's use of pointillism create very structured and static masterpieces from thousands of dots.

The depth of wood mosaics creates the feeling of motion. This heron really seems to be flying through the air above the lake.

Visualizing Your Image as a Mosaic

As you are considering images or sketches as the basis for your piece, keep in mind that you will be constructing the image from many smaller parts. I have read that our brains are always in the process of constructing images. Your eyes see only color, lines, and movement, but not whole images. Your brain must then match the colors, lines, and movement to its vast neural library of patterns to "see" an image. It makes sense, then, that color, lines and movement are the main elements of my mosaics.

If you've studied art, you have heard of George Seurat, a French post-Impressionist artist who developed pointillism. His technique used thousands of small, colored dots of paint to trick the eyes into deciphering the dots as an image. My mosaics use a similar technique with wood. Instead of dots, I use many small, sculpted wood shapes that together trick the eye into beholding a particular image. In fact, because of their depth, my sculpted pieces take it one step further; they trick the eye not only into seeing whole images but also into seeing motion.

Essential Elements in Your Pattern

How do you put together so many wood shapes and make them look like something familiar? First, you must decide upon your subject matter before you can create a pattern. The points outlined in this section will give you some guidance, which I had to learn experientially.

First, consider these points as you choose your subject matter.

Excitement

My number one rule is to choose something that excites me, wakes me up in the morning, and gets me to the shop. Find or sketch an image and put it on your phone wallpaper. Leave it there and see if it still makes you happy after a week. If it does, you know you have a subject that will keep you engaged. This step also gives you the opportunity to study your image and let your mind unconsciously work on pattern ideas. When I randomly saw the iconic photo

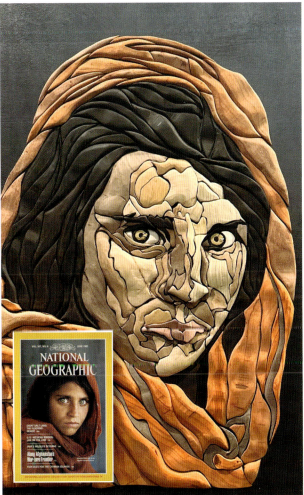

Sometimes you know immediately that you have the right subject, as I did with the Afghan Girl from *National Geographic's* June 1985 issue.

Chapter 2: Pattern Creation

of the Afghan girl from *National Geographic's* June 1985 issue, I knew immediately I would recreate her haunting expression in wood. I put the photo on my phone wallpaper and over the course of two weeks, I gained a fair idea of how I would tackle the project.

The Angle of Your Image

The best angles for making sculpted wood mosaics are approximately front facing or in profile, especially if your subject is an animal or human—anything with a face. I have found that unusual angles are difficult to translate into wood and often feel warped. Consider an image of a bird facing away from the viewer. The tail feathers in the foreground are the main identifiers of the bird, and the back of the head is in the background. The main part of the body is so foreshortened that you may not know what is going on. A profile (side) view or a more frontal view better identifies it as a bird. This art is already asking the viewer to loosen their attachments to strict interpretation, and I usually do not want to stretch the imagination across the line into confusion.

If you look at Frida Kahlo on page 30, you can see that she's front facing, although she is so recognizable, I might have enjoyed and gotten away with a more unusual pose. The wolf (page 26) is directly front facing. The Aussie shown below is a commissioned piece of a family pet and while I did ask the clients for profile or front-facing photographs, I ended up choosing a slightly off-center, whimsical pose. This one decision represented hours of reconfiguring mosaic pieces. Clearly, I do not always

This guitar is mostly front facing, which keeps the proportions looking correct while allowing the side of the guitar to show and add depth to the piece.

A slightly off-center pose, as seen with this Aussie pet portrait, can work even if it is not strictly front facing.

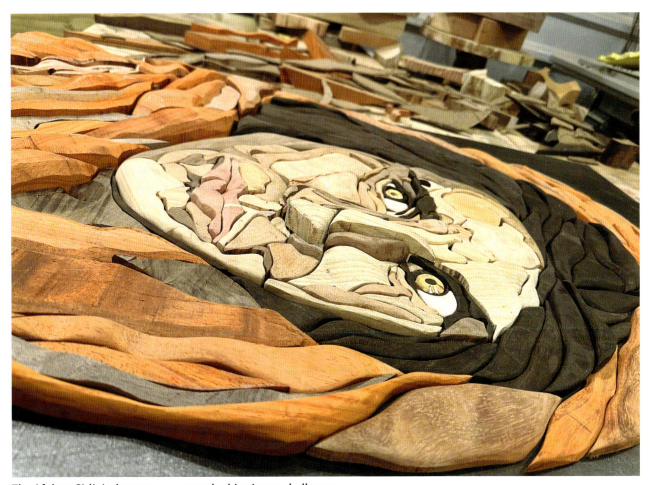

The Afghan Girl's in-between pose made this piece a challenge.

follow my own guidelines, and sometimes that works out!

The Afghan Girl is not front facing or profile either; but her face is directed somewhere solidly in between. This more solid but difficult angle was a good challenge that I felt ready for. I was so fully invested and excited throughout the process that I tackled her complexities like a dog thrown a particularly delicious bone with meat bits still on it. This fervor eventually allowed me to succeed. So, while these cautionary words are a recommendation, always follow your own intuition, feel excitement about your project, and know your skill level!

Contrast

It's easier if you choose a high-contrast image, meaning that there are areas within the image or drawing that are distinctly different from one another.

For instance, a pale face seen in deep shadows has more contrast than a pale face in bright sunlight. Those tonal differences in the shadowed face give you more broken-up areas to work with for creating your pattern. You can use your phone's photo-editing tools to create higher contrast in your image to bring out subtleties that help in pattern-making.

Frida was such a joy to make because she naturally has high-contrast areas—black hair, fair face, colorful flowers, red lips and cheeks. Because the majority of her face is pale, I created areas of naturally falling shadows to break up the all-white wood.

Much more difficult are images that have vast areas with little contrast. The Aussie (see opposite page) presented this difficulty for me because she is mostly white, hence her name, Blizzard. I picked up some subtle areas of shadowing and amped up the

The contrast of the dark walnut and the white maple, plus the patterning, create the texture of water. Even though there is only blue in the background, we understand it to be water.

contrast by using darker wood against the whitish wood. This allowed me to break up the mass of white fur. Often, by zooming in on the image, you can distinguish subtle light variations. I also could have used a maple board with ambrosia markings to create random contrast, but I instead wanted to place the shadows more intentionally.

Texture

Texture in wood mosaic art isn't about what you can feel to the touch—it's about what the eye experiences. Visual texture brings depth, movement, and emotional tone to a piece. In such a rigid medium, texture becomes your language of expression. And you have three powerful tools at your disposal: grain, color variation, and contrast.

Grain as Texture

Wood grain is nature's textural fingerprint. A tight, fine grain like some mahogany or holly creates a more solid look; a strongly grained wood like tigerwood or wood with colorful markings, such as ambrosia maple, adds texture along with depth, movement, and strong lines.

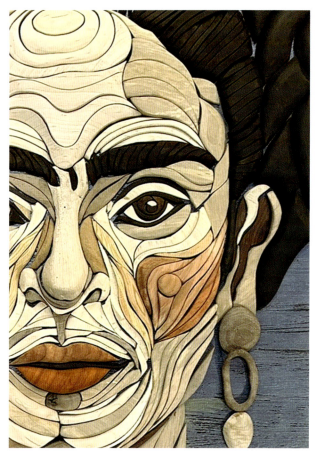

The contrast between Frida's lips, cheeks, and hair made those sections easier to design. Her face was more challenging, although the shadows helped to define different areas of her face.

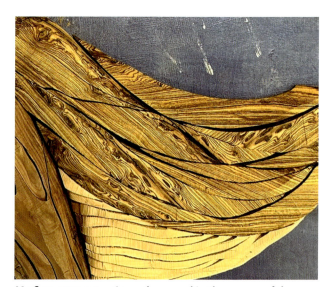

My first attempt, using zebrawood in the curves of the whale, created an unwanted geometric appearance, which I solved by using walnut instead (see the finished piece on the opposite page).

30   Making Magnificent Wood Art

Adding walnut in the curves avoided the geometric areas, and filling the frame with the whale helped capture the essence of the subject and its enormous size.

Color Variation

Even within a single wood species, you'll find subtle shifts in tone: cool and warm areas, streaks of honey or shadow, fungus shadows of blue. This variation brings life, warmth, and a type of realism where everything we view is through subtle shifts in tone and shadow. Those shifts in the way light hits the subject are texture itself. And it's not about finding "matching" pieces—it's about letting the natural variety tell the story. That's what keeps a piece from looking mechanical.

Definition

Your pattern defines the structure of your image, whether that is feathers on a bird wing, leaves on a tree, or folds in fabric. Those fine gaps between pattern pieces are like sketches from a pencil. All these thin, dark gaps create contrast between each piece and helps up see the "sketch." All of them together in a whole pattern creates a huge amount of texture. So,

Photo Credit: Kent Corley Photography

You can zoom in on a tree because the viewer does not need the whole tree to know that it is a tree.

Chapter 2: Pattern Creation **31**

if you were to use just a single species of wood and create an entire mosaic, the pattern alone will ensure a certain amount of texture and "feel." I use several other defining techniques to create texture; by placing contrasting wood tones adjacent to each other or using two or three different grain types either adjacent or within the same mosaic, all create textural interest.

Example

I was completely obsessed with sea life for a few months and knew I would eventually make a whale. What I did not realize from an artistic standpoint is how amorphous their shapes are and how little texture they actually have. We have such a romance with these gigantic mammals that I forgot they actually appear as smooth giant lumps floating in water, lacking much texture or variation. (Which is exactly how I felt when I was pregnant, so I can relate.)

Normally I would just avoid this kind of project. Realizing that it might be a challenge that makes its way to the burn pile in six months, I went for broke and used wood that has both variations in color and wood that has strong horizontal grain lines to help symbolize the striations in the whale and break up the smooth, amorphous areas. The underbelly of a whale is usually pale, so I used a white maple that had some areas of dark discoloration that broke up this big white area and almost looks like a textural shadow cast by the water. The top of a real whale has skin folds and ridges, which I mimicked with the strong grain lines of zebrawood, giving the pattern lots of horizontal lines. This is very tricky to do using the strongly linear lines of zebrawood because the whale's body is slightly curved. I had to insert some walnut where any curves happened; otherwise, trying to make the zebrawood stripes fit in that area looked geometrically off, as you can see with my first attempt.

I wanted his size to feel almost overwhelming, so I filled the frame with mostly whale. I think it turned out well mostly because these choices of wood broke up the areas of color and you can feel this giant creature floating in the blue paint.

This forest mosaic had to be large to keep the individual pieces large enough to work with.

This turtle mosaic could have been a very zoomed-in portrait because it has plenty of interest, and it would be easy to tell that it's a turtle. However, I wanted to capture some of the other elements of the turtle and opted to keep the whole subject in the sculpture.

Zooming In or Out

Deciding how close or far away you want your subject to be is a big artistic consideration. With the whale (page 31), I kept it big and zoomed out only slightly for obvious reasons. A whale also needs a few surrounding cues, like blue water, to give it contextual meaning. However, a tree could be zoomed in close so that you see only portions of it because we do not need the whole tree to know it is a tree.

Another reason not to zoom out too far is that when objects are too far away, details are lost. This can mean that the pieces become too small to work with; therefore, you lose details. The forest mosaic (opposite page) had to be physically quite large because the perspective is so zoomed out. Even so, the mosaic pieces were very small.

The turtle (opposite page) could have been zoomed in to include only the head and a portion of the shell or some other interesting close-up view, but I wanted to create a floating effect by using the space around it for painted water and sculpted coral. Also, how about that honeycomb patterning on the fin? Not at all a realistic fin pattern, but it worked. I did not create depth variations, since the fin is smooth, but I wanted it to represent the real turtle's coloring on its fin by cutting out these honeycomb shapes.

One of my herons is up close and fills the space completely. This piece on page 124 feels so thick, tactile, and feathery because of its up-close presence. Another heron piece (page 117) is further away and because of that, it has more context around it, like water lilies and the horizon, giving it a stronger story while the actual heron becomes less of a presence.

Remember that your wood mosaic is the star of the whole art piece. The painted backer board is the supporting cast, so you want enough of your beautiful wood mosaic to fully own the space and not force the paint to become more important than it is. Balancing this is key.

The heron on top feels thick, tactile, and feathery because it's up close. The heron on bottom concentrates on the whole subject and its motion, in part, because it is further away.

Methods for Drawing a Pattern

Now that you have taken all the essential elements into account and have chosen your subject, you're ready to create the actual pattern for your mosaic. There are two main ways to create a pattern: sketching your own design or tracing. You can also go without a pattern, which will also be discussed.

Making Your Own Sketch

You can sketch or draw an image from your imagination or combine elements from several photos. I usually sketch something from my imagination after browsing through tons of photos online to generate a whole idea. Honestly, my imagination is probably a composite of everything I have seen and thought was really cool. After viewing lots of photos, I will have something in mind and will sketch the general outline of the image from a photo or two and fill the rest in by hand with features I have compiled in my head.

Tracing from a Photo

You can literally trace directly from an enlarged photo that is not copyrighted to make your pattern. I use a projector that connects wirelessly to my phone, and then project my photos to the exact size I want onto paper that is taped to the wall. I then trace the major details, a few minor details, and dark and light

Because the profile of his face was mostly dark brown, I looked closely at the photos and saw veins on this horse's face; plus, I referenced other horses and discovered prominent veins. They broke up the solid brown area, and I followed them to create a pattern on the face.

I find that a projector connected to my phone is the easiest method for creating patterns from my photos and sketches.

I worked the trunk of this tree without a pattern, taking advantage of the interesting, natural grain of the board.

34   Making Magnificent Wood Art

areas. I label the areas as dark, light, and medium for later reference. I even use the projector with my own sketches to enlarge them and to figure out what details I want to keep or discard for the pattern.

Making Your Mosaic Without a Pattern

Strictly speaking, you do not absolutely need to have a pattern (although, it helps a lot). Mandalas lend themselves to this more free-flowing style because they are unique and can be composed of any kind of repeating shape around a center. Actually, this is how I make my mandalas; I build the pieces from a circular center piece and create the shapes to fit as I go. I also use this method with trees. I draw the outline of a trunk on a large piece of interesting-grain lumber, cut out the outline, and then cut it into mosaic pieces based on those grain lines. I cut around knots and follow wavy grain lines to showcase them as part of the trunk growth.

To be fair, it takes some time before you can freehand the design without first having a pattern. However, most of my patterns become suggestions, as I *always* deviate from the pattern and do what the wood and the image are telling me to do in the moment.

Sketch marks, as in this tree, give you information about the grain direction and the shape and size of your interior mosaic pieces.

This sketch of a wolf provided better and simpler information than a photograph, making the pattern I needed to create more apparent.

My sketch of a whale led me to focus on the deep horizontal belly lines and the lines that follow the upper side of the whale.

Chapter 2: Pattern Creation

The neck feathers are separate from the body feathers. I achieved this look by slightly overlapping the neck feathers where the body feathers begin. This way, there is the indication that they are separate without a real gap.

Tips for Refining Your Pattern

Now comes the true artistry where you decide how to deconstruct the interior of the outlined image into mosaic pieces. This can be an almost entirely subjective process—you could even just use dots of wood from a cut dowel rod! The breakdown you choose is without rules. This next section contains tips for the process that I use and guidelines to remember. Sometimes it's less of a process and more of an intuitive guide that only hits home after the wood is cut and the pattern I originally made feels wrong! Then, I go back to the "drawing board" with more knowledge and intuition about how to create the patterning. Instead of being frustrated, I look forward to these "breakthroughs" and stay flexible so that I do not miss them.

Follow the Sketch Lines

Sketches give so much information and are a great way to create a pattern. A sketch is composed of distinct lines and marks that help you figure out good ways to deconstruct your image. For instance, when sketching a tree trunk, your pencil will normally sketch up and down as opposed to left and right. The lines give you a clue that you can create your pattern by using random, straightish vertical lines fairly close together. Exceptions to this are aspen or birch trees, which have horizonal patterns.

I sketched the whale before I even dared to create the pattern to get a feel for it. The sketch showed

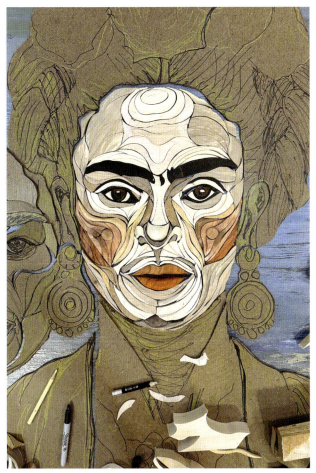

This mosaic of Frida Kahlo features curvy shapes to give realistic shading and definition to her face.

The angular nature of the pieces in the Afghan Girl mosaic reflects the harshness of her life and captures the realistic shading in the photograph.

deep horizontal belly lines and many lines that follow the upper side of the whale, without getting lost in all the other details.

The sketch of the horse on page 34 shows shading in the form of lines. The direction that I drew the lines gave me clues about the direction my pattern cut lines needed to follow. I sketched the wolf to understand the fur and discovered that the fur radiates in all directions from the nose. The fur above the nose radiates up, the fur under the nose radiates down, and the fur on the sides radiates out to the sides. I then patterned the wood pieces to look like they are directional. Obviously, it would be too difficult to pattern each individual hair, so I instead patterned many clumps of hair or tufts to look like a mass of fur. A photo of a wolf might have had too

many other elements and not been simple enough to see this right away. The sketch simplifies the image into lines that you can use for creating a pattern.

If you do not feel confident with sketching, you can search the internet for sketched images. I do this all the time. Maybe you want to create a pattern for a turtle. Viewing sketches online could help you see lines, shading, and shapes more clearly and help you understand where to break down the pattern even further. This is not cheating at all. Sometimes a different perspective can help you see the details in a new way. Applications like Sketchify on Canva or ChatGPT, which generate a sketch from a photo, may help in this process (see Tools on page 10), although I have not used them myself.

Chapter 2: Pattern Creation   **37**

Mimic Real Life

Especially for wildlife, I spend time studying my subjects so that I know what helps make them look realistic. When I create a wood mosaic of a bird, I know it will mean patterning multiple layers of feathers from studying photographs and individual feathers. If you look at a real heron's neck, you'll see that it is composed of tiny feathers. However, they would be way too small to make in wood and too smooth to pattern them as feathers. Instead, I drew lines along the neck for the eye to follow that mimics the directional flow of the feathers. I made sure to use curvy lines because straight lines do not often occur in nature. Curvy lines cause the eye to see movement or flow.

In human faces, it is important to capture the prominent features and shadows to have realism in the mosaic. Look at the ways I patterned the faces of Frida Kahlo and the Afghan Girl. Frida's cheeks and forehead are almost like a topographical map because she is front facing and protruding cheeks, forehead, and nose are less apparent than when in profile. Also, her delicate smooth skin needed texture. For that reason, I needed to give the illusion of peaks to her cheeks and forehead. I patterned distinct pieces curving in the shape of the cheekbones and the forehead that allowed me to gradually increase the height of the wood in those areas. Her pattern pieces are also very flowy, which I did intentionally to reflect her feminine beauty and artistic nature, while also trying to convey the dark side to her personality.

The pattern of the Afghan Girl's face is, by contrast, much more angular. The pieces are a bit geometric, conveying the harshness of her life and surroundings. I patterned the pieces by observing the light shading on her face. Each different wood color is where the light created differing shades on her face. I could have made those more organically curvy, but again, I chose the harsher angles. Because her face is slightly in profile to the light source, I had an easy time finding shadows.

The random, wavelike pattern of the dragon's tendrils creates a feeling of motion that's inherent in the pattern.

Here you can see how the curving, wavy leaf patterns create the sense of motion.

Create a Feeling of Motion

The feeling of motion mostly comes from the sculpting step (addressed in the next chpater on page 45), but I need to touch lightly on the pattern creation here because there are times when you create motion within the pattern itself. There is an obvious example in the tendrils of the dragon, which come off in a random, wavelike pattern. Another example of motion created with the pattern is in a tree with curving, waving leaves (see above).

Create Depth

Depth creation really belongs in the sculpting section, but it's helpful during the pattern stage to mark the depth for reference later. I often mark the areas that protrude toward me, the areas that fall away from me, and then everything in between. By doing this, I know approximately how to cut the wood to create the best and most representative differences in depth within the image, translated in wood thickness, that reflects real life. This part is especially important with faces since they must be the most precise.

Create Variation

Just as great music needs to have high and low notes or slow and fast rhythms instead of one long, medium style, so do mosaics. The listener craves the crescendo, but without low tones, the crescendo cannot build. If your mosaic will have a lot of similarly sized pieces or if it will be mostly one color, you'll need to create variation in another aspect of the design. If my mosaic is mostly made up of small pieces, then it needs lots of wood color variation or sculpting depth differences. If the mosaic has a monochromatic color theme, such as all cherry wood, then it needs lots of differently sized pieces to be more evocative. Sometimes I do not follow this rule, but it works for me most of the time.

I love the effect of this monochromatic tree. Using similarly colored wood species, I shifted the focus from color to the distinct shapes of the leaves and the thick, tactile trunk. A smooth, monochromatic background aided this as well.

Chapter 3: Techniques

In this section, I'll cover the basic techniques of making a backer board, preparing the pattern, and sculpting the mosaic pieces. These are the techniques you'll need for almost any sculpted wood mosaic that you undertake. Be sure to refer back to this section as needed when you are working through the projects.

Making a Backer Board

The backer board is basically the flat background where you mount and glue your mosaic. However, this backer board is also a part of the art, so creative thought needs to go into how you paint this background. In this book, we will use ½" (1.3cm) sanded plywood for the backer board. You could also use metal, glass, or any flat surface you wish, as long as your adhesive is suitable for adhering your mosaic pieces to your backer board material.

Painting the backer board is one way to make your mosaic stand out. Since wood in its natural state is matte and textured, contrasting it with paints that have a luminous shimmer, such as metallic paint, differentiates it from your mosaic. I also find that using colors not often found in wood, such as true black, silver, blue, violets, and greens, help set off the mosaic nicely. However, paint that meets the "paint" criteria (see page 14) can be used and you should choose what suits your own taste. In addition, layering different colors and allowing base colors to show through can create a 3D effect that pairs well with the wood mosaic.

Colors not often found in wood, such as green, help set off a mosaic nicely.

Layering different colors and allowing base colors to show through can create a 3D effect that pairs well with the wood mosaic.

Backer Board Preparation

Here are the steps to prepare the backer board.

1. Cut the backer board to the size specified in the project materials section. Choose sanded plywood that is not scratched or blemished. Before cutting, tape down the cut lines with foil tape to prevent splintering.

42   Making Magnificent Wood Art

2. Sand the backer board sides with 180-grit sandpaper followed by 240 grit. Sand the front edges and round slightly.

Preparing the Pattern

The patterns in this book have a recommended size for your project. Sizing up or down is optional but usually not recommended beyond a 10% increase or decrease. First, see what your project requires—whether it is one or two hardboards, one or two copies of the pattern—know the sizing, and then check back to this section to prepare these requirements. Note: Photocopy the patterns on pages 95–98, or download and print them by following the QR code.

Scan for downloadable patterns.

There are two ways to prepare the patterns in this book. In method 1, you will need to have access to a printer that can custom enlarge the paper pattern (such as a copy shop). In method 2, you will need an inexpensive projector to enlarge a photo of the paper pattern.

3. Paint the front and sides of the backer board with metallic paint or the paint of your choice. Use a 2" (5.1cm) brush, small roller, or gloved hands. Apply two coats according to paint directions. Alternatively, layer different paint colors by applying the first color, drying, and then applying another color and wiping off in some areas. Repeat with different colors. Dry between coats, and allow the board to dry thoroughly before applying the mosaic.

Method 1

1. Print copies of the patterns to the recommended size.
2. Cut sheet(s) of your hardboard to the exact size or slightly larger than your paper patterns and place the hardboard, smooth side up, on your worktable.
3. Spray the hardboard sheet(s) and cover them completely with adhesive.
4. Immediately center and press one paper pattern onto each hardboard sheet.
5. Lift and smooth out any wrinkles.

Method 2

In this method, an image from your phone or computer is connected (through Bluetooth) to an image projector and projected onto a piece of hardboard the size of your project. I used this approach to produce my patterns for all the projects in this book.

1. Take a photo of the book pattern on your phone or scan it to a digital file on your phone or computer.
2. Cut a piece(s) of hardboard that is same size as your project backer board. Tape one of them onto a wall or against the back of a chair without leaning it.
3. Project the image onto the full size of the hardboard pattern. Make sure the projector is in line with the hardboard; if the projector is tilted

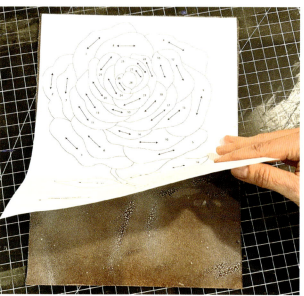

up or down, left or right, it will distort the pattern onto your hardboard. One way to tell if there is distortion: when you focus the magnification of the projector, one part of the image remains out of focus. Readjust until the whole pattern is in equal focus. If your hardboard is larger than the pattern, trace a thick black sharpie line to outline the pattern dimensions, then project your image within those lines.

4. Trace the pattern directly onto the hardboard. If you need a second hardboard copy or a paper copy, mount the second hardboard or suitably large paper to the same spot on the wall (without moving the projector) and repeat the process. You now have hardboard patterns and/or paper patterns to begin your project.

Sculpting the Wood

It is this sculpting part of the process that most brings my sculptures to life. Because I knew so little about woodcraft and wood saws, I began to use my bandsaw and scroll saw as carving tools, passing the wood through the saw at different angles. The actual mechanical techniques I use are not special or revolutionary. Most carving tools accomplish the same task. Instead, it is the multitude of creative and personal decisions in creating a pattern, what wood to choose, and how and where to sculpt that truly forms my sculptures.

Remember, we are not actually recreating an image into a full 3D wood sculpture, and it may take a bit of trial and error to get the sculpture right. As such, you must periodically view your work from a distance and see for yourself if the illusion of depth is working.

Before we launch into the actual sculpting method, I want you to understand that by the time you get to the sculpting stage of your mosaic, you have made many sculpting decisions already. In fact, four primary opportunities present themselves for you to shape and sculpt your wood mosaic. Let's review them in the approximate order these decisions are made as you build your mosaic.

The first time in the process that you make sculpting decisions is during pattern creation as you deconstruct the image into parts.

Choosing wood thickness to define the highs and lows of your piece will aid you before you begin the actual sculpting process.

Chapter 3: Techniques **45**

The thin, ebony wood for the dragon's mouth conveys its depth to the viewer.

The left side of the Afghan Girl's face near the hairline has darker wood to tell the observer that it's further in the background.

Creating the pattern. The first opportunity is through the creation of a pattern or the "deconstruction" of your image into a unique arrangement of pieces (as discussed in the previous chapter). In terms of importance, this one is the creative foundation of all the following three and is the two-dimensional shaping and sculpting of your mosaic.

Choosing the thickness of wood. The second opportunity is in choosing different thicknesses of wood. In the appropriate areas of your mosaic, you can create high and low areas to suggest greater depth, create perspective, and thereby enhance the third dimension in the observer's experience.

Selecting wood colors. The third way to shape your mosaic is with wood color. Placing two different

Wood color can represent both color changes and depth changes in your subject, as in this heron wing.

wood colors together that change from light to dark can imply depth, although it does not have to. For an obvious example, inside the dragon mouth (see opposite page), I used a thin piece of ebony wood. In this case, I used both wood thickness (or thinness) and color to create the illusion of the deep dark mouth of the dragon. Less obviously, on the left side of the Afghan Girl's face near the hairline (see opposite page), I use darker wood to tell the observer that it's not as prominent there; that it is further in the background. That area is also shaded, but depth often is announced by shading, so they sometimes go hand in hand. Sometimes, wood color represents the actual colors of your image in addition to different levels of depth, such as different rows of feathers in a wing (see above).

Sculpting each piece. Finally, the fourth and most impactful is sculpting the surface of each piece, keeping the bottom intact to preserve the original shape. I call this the 3D sculpting aspect of my wood mosaics. When you first cut your pattern into wood, the surface of each piece is flat and only two dimensional. This third dimension can be sculpted to represent texture, structure, movement, and even emotional expression. Imagine leaving out this step! You would miss the opportunity to turn an essentially flat and static mosaic into an expressive and alive sculpture.

Chapter 3: Techniques

Notice how the left tree (which is an early piece and is not sculpted at all) looks primitive compared to the piece on the right (with the sculpting). Depth, expression, and motion have entered the equation.

The Sculpting Method

Imagine you are sculpting a heart shape into a wood relief (a relief is any work in which the figures project from a supporting background, usually a two-dimensional surface). You would begin with a thick, flat panel of wood and use carving tools to chisel away the excess material to reveal the heart. Now that you have finished the relief, I want you to imagine cutting that panel with the carved heart into pieces and fitting them back together like a jigsaw puzzle. You now have a mosaic of a heart in relief. In this section, I am describing this same process to you, except in reverse. We are cutting the flat wood surface into pieces *first*, and then carving/sculpting each piece into a heart. I find it helpful to think about it backward when sculpting each piece and asking, "What would this piece look like if it had been carved/sculpted first, as part of a relief, and then cut out?" I mentally use this process for every single sculpture I create.

In essence, treating these mosaics like a relief carving in reverse is a cheat code that will get you started making simple mosaics. As you do more of these, you will progress in your own style.

Every sculpture is basically a new opportunity to become better at the illusion of depth. When I started, my pieces were very simple with just basic sculpting. With time and experimentation, I have introduced more complex patterning and sculpting that has created more visually interesting and illusionary mosaic sculptures.

In this section, I use example mosaics to explain how I sculpted the various parts and why I chose to do it that way. Each sculpture you do will be unique and will present different types of sculpting opportunities and challenges.

Both of these photos are examples of reliefs. Mount Rushmore (left) is called a "high" relief, similar to sculpting with really thick wood and getting a more tactile prominent sculpture. The sculpture from the Parthenon (right) is an example of a "low" relief—still sculptural but more delicate. It does not have as much depth or 3D effect.

Here is one of my early works before I began sculpting the third dimension. These pieces are flat and quite static.

Chapter 3: Techniques

Example 1: Sculpting for Texture and Motion

Most of my nature-themed sculptures have slightly random variations sculpted into the surface of almost every piece of the mosaic. Is there a reason for this? Yes, absolutely. Nature isn't laser perfect. Feathers are ruffled, leaves are misshapen, the wind flutters leaves, tree trunks are not straight or smooth, whales aren't shaped like perfect torpedoes, petals are curved inexactly.

I intentionally make random curvy cuts that are (usually) very shallow, wave-like irregularities along the top surface of each mosaic piece, like wind across a lake. This wavelike sculpting of the surface prevents an area from appearing as a solid mass and introduces a feeling of motion.

Wavy cuts are made by turning the pattern piece on its side and cutting a shallow wave into the top surface. As I sculpt for depth and overall resemblance to the image, I add this variation for texture and a sense of movement without interfering with that resemblance.

Example 2: Sculpting for Depth and Shape

Most sculpting of the mosaic involves creating higher and lower points on the top surface by choosing what depth to cut off and where to cut in places where the image has real-life depth differences. The thickness of your wood allows this sculpting cut to be either dramatic highs and lows or more delicate and shallow depth differences. Thicker wood creates a more impactful illusion of depth by allowing for higher highs and lower lows.

Within each particular sculpture, I locate areas that project the highest into the 3D plane, decide how thick I want that projection, and choose an appropriate wood either for that area or for the entire sculpture if there are many high areas. It is easier to cut wood away than to start with something too thin, so I usually give myself the freedom to cut as much away as I need to by starting with thick wood.

Example 3: High Points

Each sculpted piece must fit into the overall sculpture so that it makes sense with the other pieces around it. Here are three examples for identifying the high points and then sculpting those pieces to seamlessly flow into the surrounding sections.

The Afghan Girl's nose was a more complex sculpting process. Her face pattern was divided according to light and dark areas, but those areas have different scales of depth and curvature, especially the nose. I took each piece, studied it against the photo, and determined exactly how that area curved and how deep it was. Then, I used the scroll saw to gradually shave away excess wood to reveal those curves and dips.

All the pieces above the snout on the wolf are cut so they curve similarly from high near the snout to low near the eyes, to represent the prominence and symmetry of the nose.

For the Aussie, the white areas on either side of the nose were sculpted by cutting a curve into the surface of the wood piece that began at the highest point and ended at a lower point near the edge of the face, at the cheek area. These nose pieces required a convex cut to give the illusion of a bulbous shape, and each one was cut similarly in keeping with the pattern. Also, I needed to know how thick I wanted the facial fur pieces to be because the lowest point of each nose piece must end at the same height as the cheek pieces.

Example 4: Layered Depth and Motion
This heron is an exceptional example of sculpting with thicker wood to create the illusion of greater depth and deep curves for motion. It also illustrates blending between different woods for layered features.

The bottom wing feathers are closer to the observer, and they project into the 3D plane at the highest point. For that reason, I used really thick wood for this area. The feathers just above them are slightly further away from the foreground, so the wood is slightly thinner to create that effect. The feathers at the top of the wing were made with slightly thinner wood than the middle layer and rounded at the top edge to mimic the top edge of the wing.

I used different wood for each layer of feathers to accentuate their separateness. I sculpted the surface of each feather within each layer similarly, but with variation (see Example 1: Sculpting for Texture and Motion on page 50) because each feather is not static. My sculpting cut created a curved shape that allowed the feathers in each layer to fit slightly underneath the layer above it. This technique gives the illusion of the feathers being layered, and it hides the top of each wood feather. I cut the bottom layer of feathers to flutter or dish out dramatically and raggedly as I imagined that they were a bit uneven and bent out from the wind.

Example 5: Half-Barrel Shaping

This tree trunk and whale are simple examples of sculpting the surface of each mosaic piece to create an overall shape. For subjects like these, I use a half-barrel shape to give the illusion of roundness.

For tree trunks, I usually trace the pattern of the main trunk onto a single wood board. Once the pattern is cut out, I sculpt the pieces at the outermost left and right sides of the tree trunk, the lowest points. These are the thinnest, so I turn those pieces on their side and cut off the surface longitudinally. At the same time as I am cutting for depth, I cut for texture and motion. That means I am cutting a wave-like motion into it, with irregular highs and lows. Then, I mark the next unsculpted, adjacent piece where the sculpted one meets it. I repeat the process of cutting, except I cut this one a bit higher. Once I reach the middle of the trunk, the highest point, I do the same on the other side of the trunk. Basically, you are cutting and sculpting as needed to get a half-barrel shape, while implementing the natural random variance that creates motion and texture.

The approach to sculpting the whale is almost identical. All outside edge pieces of the whale were sculpted down to gradually fall away to the backer board, giving the illusion of roundedness.

Chapter 3: Techniques

Example 6: Fur

To get realistic-looking fur, you need to decide the height, cut the waves in the surfaces of the pieces, and then mark each unsculpted, adjacent piece to match the general thickness of the sculpted piece beside it.

Example 7: Shaping Faces

When sculpting faces, pay attention to the bone structures and contours of the face. These will guide you in finding the high and low points of your sculpture. The cheekbones are often a critical area, so we'll look at two examples here.

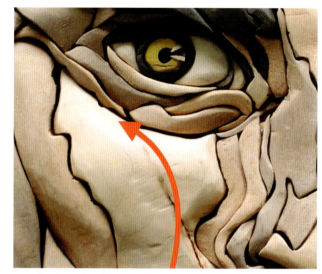

Let's look at the cheeks of the Afghan Girl. To allow the cheekbone to rise higher within a single pattern piece, I cut away or sculpt down the outer one-third of the surface of the cheekbone piece with the scroll or band saw to gradually lower those areas that are just outside the most prominent part of the cheekbone.

Notice the fur pieces of the Aussie and wolf have a wave shape cut into the surface. In the pattern I produced for the wolf and the dog, starting from the nose area, the fur radiates away in all directions. To sculpt each piece, I cut a wave into the top surface in the same direction that the fur is radiating. It creates not only motion but also the illusion of the fur projecting away from the nose and off the body.

If we look at Frida Kahlo, her cheeks are patterned into curved pieces that resemble a wave. The surface of the wave pieces is cut to remain high at the cheekbone and fall away toward the side of the face and below the cheekbone.

Example 8: Sculpting Excavations

Following the similar idea of creating realistic depth changes in our mosaic, but using a different technique, you can sculpt away or excavate the interior of a single wood pattern piece to convey a deepening space or gap, as in flower petals overlapping one another. If we look down at the top of a real rose, we know each petal is a thin spoon shape that curves from the base to the surface of the rose, overlapping other similar petals. Looking at the unsculpted rose on the left, how can these flat petal shapes represent a real 3D rose? We need to sculpt the interior of each petal piece so that is gives the illusion of disappearing into the depths of the rose and gives the illusion of that spoon shape, as in the photo on the right.

I hollow the petal piece by carving away the interior excess. We want the viewer to feel the petal's high thin edge, and then the hollow curve as it drops down into the base of the rose. By turning the piece on its bottom inside edge, the sculpting cut follows the top outside edge of the piece as you cut away the interior down to the bottom inside edge, shaving off the interior bit by bit, while keeping the entire bottom intact and uncut. The bottom of each mosaic piece holds the original shape of the piece before it is sculpted. This original shape is necessary to keep the pattern true. Therefore, the bottom of the piece is never cut away or changed.

Chapter 3: Techniques

Chapter 4: Projects

For this chapter, I have selected four projects to take you through the techniques we've discussed in the previous sections and allow you to build your skills as you progress through each project. I've given you patterns to help make that part of the process easier, and I've provided you with suggested woods for the different pieces. Treat these projects less like recipes and more like living forms—meant to evolve through your hands. Shift the patterning, choose different woods, follow what feels right for you. Let the process breathe.

Floral Mandala Mosaic

The mandala mosaic is a great introductory project because it has a more straightforward sculpt than the other projects. Plus, the mandala pieces are not meant to fit together perfectly; there are intentional gaps. This easier entry point allows you to get used to the sculpting technique before taking on other projects.

As a bonus, this pattern offers an exciting opportunity to use a great variety of colors and grains of wood. The mandala has a repeating pattern around a center circular piece. This internal pattern repeats five times around the center, so you will be cutting each similar repeating piece five times with the same wood species. I say "similar," not identical, because the beauty of handmade creations is in the uniqueness of each piece.

You can either follow the recommendation for wood species, use a different species of wood for each unique piece within the repeating pattern (that is 19 different wood species!), or choose whatever wood

Materials and Tools

- 1 square of painted backer board, 17" x 17" (43.2 x 43.2cm) (see page 42 for more information)
- 2 squares of 17" x 17" (43.2 x 43.2cm) hardboard with paper pattern glued on or pattern traced directly onto hardboards from projector (see page 44 for more information)
- 24 square inches (154.8 sq cm) of 1" or 1¼" (2.5 or 3.2cm) thick boards of ash, mahogany, cypress, padauk, pink ivory*, sapele*
- 48 square inches (309.7 sq cm) of 1" or 1¼" (2.5 or 3.2cm) thick boards of cedar, tigerwood, maple, and walnut
- Fine-tip Sharpie or sharpened pencil
- Scroll saw with universal blades #3 and #7
- Oscillating drum sander with ¾" (19mm) drum, 180 and 240 grits
- Sanding mop with 400 grit or sandpaper for hand-sanding, 400 grit
- Clear construction adhesive (dispensed with a caulk gun) or viscous CA glue
- Acrylic clear nonyellowing exterior finish for water and UV protection

Wood species suggested for each pattern piece:

- 0 (center piece) cedar
- 1 maple
- 2 walnut
- 3 cedar
- 4 padauk
- 5 tigerwood
- 6 walnut
- 7 tigerwood
- 8 walnut
- 9 pink ivory
- 10 cypress
- 11 padauk
- 12 mahogany
- 13 maple
- 14 ash
- 15 cedar
- 16 sapele
- 17 walnut

*If you don't have pink ivory, you can substitute African mahogany or any red or pink wood. For sapele, you can substitute walnut or mahogany.

1. Mark the pattern as shown in the photo. These five sections represent the repeating pattern in the mandala.

you have on hand and repeat them strategically throughout the mandala.

This project allows you to use all the small scraps of wood that you cannot bear to throw out. Perhaps you do not have a wood-hoarding problem like I do. If you do save wood scraps, then this project will, for better or worse, reinforce that habit.

Pattern on page 95.

free space to keep pattern in place

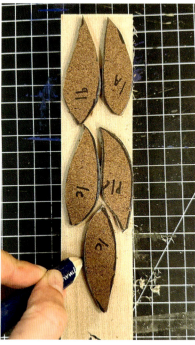

2. Carefully cut the hardboard pattern along the lines you marked in Step 1 with a #3 scroll saw blade. You are cutting out the a, b, c, d, and e groupings first. Reassemble the pattern on the prepared backer board. *Note: Set aside the second hardboard pattern as a backup.*

3. Cut the pieces out of the hardboard. One section at a time, cut out each individual pattern piece and return each piece to its place within the pattern. Save the outside "free space" and fit it back in the pattern to keep the mosaic pieces in place as you build it.

4. Align pattern pieces 1a–e on the wood you've chosen. Make sure the grain runs in the same direction for all of them. It does not matter what direction the grain runs, as long as it is the same for each of the 5 pieces.

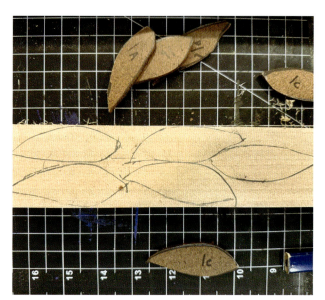

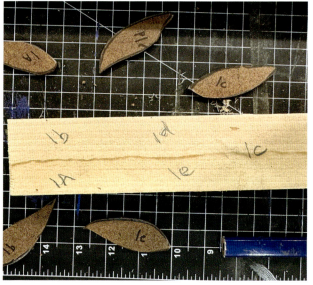

5. Trace the outline of the pattern pieces onto the wood with a fine-point Sharpie or pencil. Pull the pen tightly against the pattern piece as you mark. Turn the wood board over and label the bottom of each pattern piece.

Making Magnificent Wood Art

6. Cut the outlined wood shapes 1a–e on the scroll saw with a #7 blade. Cut along the inside edge of your tracing.

7. Place all five of the newly cut wood pieces onto the backer board in their numbered places within the pattern. Set the 1a–e hardboard pattern pieces aside. *Note: If one of the wood pieces fits poorly, check it against the pattern piece and either trim or recut.* Repeat this process for pieces 2 to 20 (all pieces a–e), using the assigned wood species for each number with its five pieces. Finally, cut the center circular piece, 21, as well.

8. Begin sculpting each piece on the scroll saw with a #7 blade. One at a time, beginning with pieces 1a–1e, turn each piece on its side on the scroll saw table and cut off the top surface in a wavelike motion using the scroll saw.

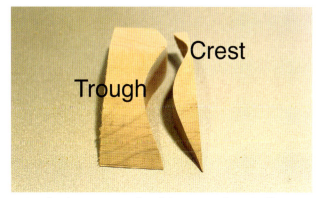

9. Cut the deepest troughs of the waves about halfway into the piece (from the top surface) and the top of the waves near the top surface of the piece. You can begin your cut at the deepest point, or you can begin to cut near the top. However you choose to cut, make similar cuts for the entire five-piece grouping. Note: You need to hold the mandala piece you are sculpting firmly down on the scroll saw table since the piece is resting on its curved side and is not very stable.

Chapter 4: Projects   Floral Mandala Mosaic

10. Return the sculpted piece to its place in the pattern, checking the bottom to identify it. Repeat this process for 1a–1e.

If you use a band saw that has some chatter (cut lines), you will need to sand with the 180-grit sandpaper on the drum sander. If you use a scroll saw and have a smooth, shiny cut, you can probably skip the heavy sanding and go over it with the 200-grit drum or mop sander.

11. Repeat this process for the rest of the 20 groupings of five (a–e). For the centerpiece, cut off ⅓" (8.5mm) from the top.

12. Remove one piece at a time and begin sanding. Using an oscillating drum sander fitted with a ¾" to 1" (19 to 25mm) drum and 180- to 200-grit sandpaper, sand the sides and top of each piece until the cut lines are smoothed out. Round the top edges slightly, removing the sharpness of the edge but not creating a rounded sloping edge.

13. Finish sanding each piece with 400-grit sandpaper on a mop sander or by hand. Wipe down the pieces with a microfiber cloth to remove all sawdust. Return each piece to the mosaic.

64   Making Magnificent Wood Art

14. After sanding, apply exterior UV and moisture control acrylic finish and allow it to dry. Reapply. Sand again with the mop sander or by hand with 400-grit sandpaper.

15. Remove and glue the center circular piece first. If you have trouble removing it or any pieces, you can use needle-nose pliers to remove them. Coat the bottom lightly with glue. Replace the piece and seat firmly. Then, starting from the inside to the outside pieces, cover the bottom center area of each mosaic piece moderately with glue. Avoid applying glue near the outside edges to prevent seepage.

16. Repeat with all the pieces. Leave glue to dry until set. Optional: Attach hanging device to the back and frame the piece.

Rose Reverie Mosaic

Without the sculpting method I describe for each piece in this mosaic, this rose would be flat, cartoonish, and uninspiring. With sculpting, you can feel the depth of each sculpted petal as it originates at the stem. Even though you cannot see that origin, it is implied. Each petal becomes beautifully distinct, delicately soft, and ready to pluck. They come to life. By following this step-by-step project, you will end up with a tactile, almost fragrant rose that is uniquely your art. Experiment within the parameters given and do not be afraid to abandon a piece if it just does not feel right; redo it and move forward.

Materials and Tools

- 1 square of painted backer board, 14" x 14" (35.6 x 35.6cm) (see page 42 for more information)
- 2 squares of 14" x 14" (35.6 x 35.6cm) hardboard with paper pattern glued on or pattern traced directly onto hardboards from projector (see page 44 for more information)
- Fine-tip Sharpie or sharpened pencil
- 200 square inches (0.1 sq m) of 1¼" to 1⅓" (3.2 to 3.4cm) thick cedar board for petals
- 40 square inches (258.1 sq cm) of 1¼" to 1⅓" (3.2 to 3.4cm) thick walnut wood board for stems and leaves
- Scroll saw with #5 and #7 or #9 blades, 10 to 15 TPI, or band saw with ⅛" (3.2mm) blade, 10 TPI
- Oscillating drum sander with 1" (25mm) drum, 180 and 240 grits
- Sanding mop with 400 and 600 grits or sandpaper for hand sanding, 400 and 600 grits
- Clear construction adhesive (dispensed with a caulk gun) or viscous CA glue
- Acrylic clear nonyellowing exterior finish for water and UV protection (optional)

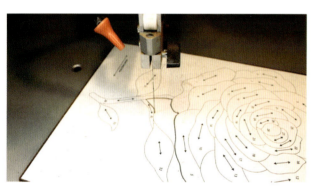

1. Cut the outline of your pattern. Follow the directions for preparing your backer board and pattern. On the scroll saw with a #3 blade, cut out the *outline only* of the rose pattern image from both hardboard patterns.

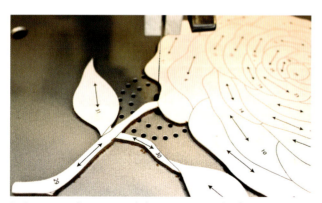

3. Separate the rose and the stem. Begin by first cutting where the stem attaches to the rose for ease of cutting.

2. Place one of the cutout hardboard patterns on your painted backer board. Set the other one aside on your workbench. This one will remain intact and be your guide during the process.

Pattern on page 96.

4. Cut out each piece of the pattern, starting from the outside and working in. As you cut out the pattern *one piece at a time*, return and reassemble each pattern piece onto the backer board. Consult the intact pattern if necessary for reassembly.

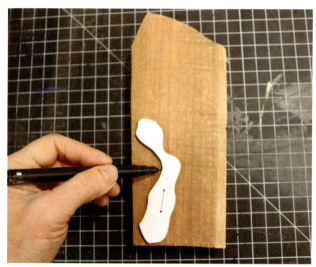

5. Pick up hardboard pattern piece #1, and position it on top of your cedar wood board. Make sure the arrows run in the same direction as the grain, and try to position your first cut as close to a corner edge as possible for less waste. Feel free to incorporate an intact knot or swirly grain. Trace with a fine-tipped Sharpie or pencil onto the wood board. Set aside.

6. Cut out the traced area on the wood board with a scroll saw or band saw, using a #7 blade. Cut on the inside edge of your traced line. Set the pattern piece aside in case you need to recut this piece.

7. Place the cutout wood petal in its proper place in the pattern on the backer board. Follow this tracing and cutting process with all the hardboard pattern pieces until the entire sculpture is cut out in your select wood and positioned on the backer board.

 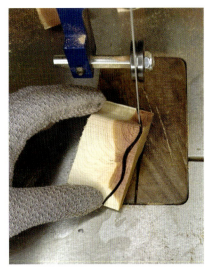 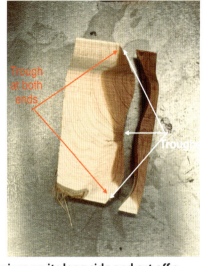

8. For the leaves and stems pattern pieces, follow the same steps by positioning them on the walnut board, tracing and cutting. Stop at this point and check for any ill-fitting petal pieces. If there are gaps bigger than ⅛" to ¼" (3.2 to 6.4mm), you may want to recut or trim the piece that is causing the gap. However, the aim is not jigsaw-puzzle perfection.

9. Starting with petal #1, turn the petal piece on its long side and cut off a portion from the top surface in a curving, organic, wavelike fashion. Cut off about ⅓" (8.5mm) at the deepest parts (trough) of the wave. Start the wavelike cut at one end of the petal at the deepest depth and end the wavelike cut at the deepest depth at the other end of the petal, so that each end of the petal tapers off. For longer pieces, the wave can have multiple troughs and peaks. Be smooth with the cut.

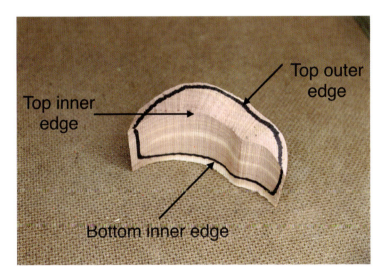 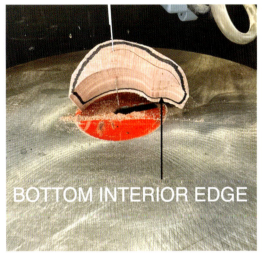

10. Working with the same petal piece, use a scroll saw to cut/excavate the interior of the petal. Rest the petal on its bottom inner edge with the intent to cut away the top inner edge.

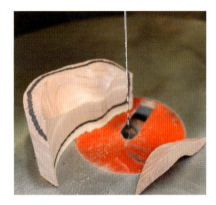
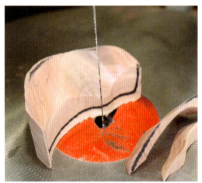

11. Follow the shape of the petal's top outer edge with your blade while gradually cutting away thin pieces from the top inner edge. With each cut, you get closer to the top outer edge and the bottom inner edge. Don't worry about perfection; any material not cut away can be sanded away at a later step. Ultimately, we are aiming for a thin petal edge at the top, gradually growing to the full-size petal at the bottom.

12. Return the sculpted petal to its proper place in the mosaic, and follow this process for sculpting each piece of the flower's petals. For the centermost piece, sand a ⅓" (8.5mm) tall slope on one side of the top of this circular center petal.

13. One at a time on the scroll saw, turn each leaf on its side and cut about ⅓" (8.5mm) from the top in a deep, wavelike pattern. Discard the top ⅓" (8.5mm) piece and return the bottom of each leaf to the mosaic.

14. Turn the stems on their sides and cut along the midline of its length in a wavelike pattern. This may include several waves. Discard the top and return the bottom piece to the mosaic.

Making Magnificent Wood Art

15. Sand the outside of the petals and the sculpted interior of the flower petals with the oscillating drum sander at 180 grit. Be careful not to take off too much with the 180 grit, but any material not cut away earlier in the sculpting step can now be sanded down and evened out. Follow up with 240 grit to smooth the entire surface and slightly round out the top edge of the petal. Finish by mop or hand sanding with 400-grit sandpaper.

16. Sand the sides and top of the leaves with the oscillating drum sander at 180 grit until the saw lines have disappeared. Round out the top edges of the leaves only slightly, keeping them fairly sharp. Repeat and smooth the entire surface with a drum or mop sander at 240 grit. Mop or hand sand with 400-grit sandpaper.

17. Sand the stems with a drum sander at 180 grit. Smooth out the saw lines on the sides of the stems and heavily round the two top long edges to create a half-barrel shape. Be careful not to take off too much material. Further smooth each piece with a 240-grit drum. Finish by mop sanding or hand sanding with 400-grit sandpaper for a smooth shine.

18. Wipe the sawdust from each piece. Then, apply two coats of acrylic clear nonyellowing exterior finish to the sides and top of each sculpture piece, according to product directions. Allow to dry. Re-sand each piece lightly with 400-grit sandpaper. (The acrylic finish will raise the grain). Center the sculpture onto the backer board. Use the intact pattern to check for correct positioning.

19. Starting at the center of the flower, one piece at a time, pick up and apply CA glue or clear construction adhesive in a thin layer on the bottom of each petal. Replace each petal gently but firmly. Continue until all petals (except the outermost layer) have been glued down. For the outermost petals, leaves, and stems, apply a thin coat of glue in the center and down the length of the piece. This ensures no glue seeps out at the edges.

Carved Canopy Mosaic

Trees are my most requested sculptural mosaic. As a result, I can make a tree without sketching a pattern first. Most of the time, at the beginning, I have no idea what it will look like—if it will have a thick, gnarly trunk or lean to one side or branch out into two trunks. The tree gradually reveals itself to me as I follow the knots or swirly grain lines and begin cutting out the trunk pattern directed, in part, by these unusual grain lines. Most of all, it's an intuitive knowing that comes after making a lot of trees!

This tree trunk is centered on a central knot, which may or may not actually exist in the wood, but patterning will make it appear to exist. The small, low branch coming off the knotted area helps create an interesting asymmetry that allows the eye to relax and enjoy. This tree's trunk is made from cedar, but if you prefer to work with a less fragile wood, use cherry, mahogany, or gum wood. All of them will produce a beautiful result.

In this project, I will tell you all the different types of wood I used for the leaves. These were all bits and pieces of wood I had around the shop. You may substitute any hardwoods you have available, even if it is a scrap piece and you only get one or two leaves from it. You might notice that the interior of the tree canopy is dark with walnut leaves and gets lighter as you extend outward into the sunshine. Any grouping of different types of wood for the leaves—even all the same wood—will work and have its own beauty. The choice is yours.

Materials and Tools

- 1 square of painted backer board, 23" x 23" (58.4 x 58.4cm) (see page 42 for more information)
- 2 squares of 23" x 23" (58.4 x 58.4cm) hardboard with paper pattern glued on or pattern traced directly onto hardboards from projector (see page 44 for more information)
- 6" x 24" (15.2 x 61cm) of approximately 1" (2.5cm) thick cedar board for trunk and leaves (or wood of your choice)
- 40 square inches (258.1 sq cm) of ¾" or 1" (1.9 or 2.5cm) thick walnut board
- 40 square inches (258.1 sq cm) of ¾" or 1" (1.9 or 2.5cm) thick soft maple
- 40 square inches (258.1 sq cm) of ¾" or 1" (1.9 or 2.5cm) thick ash or cherry
- 20 square inches (129 sq cm) of ¾" or 1" (1.9 or 2.5cm) thick cypress or heart pine
- Fine-tip Sharpie or sharpened pencil
- Tape
- Scroll saw with universal blades #5 and #7 or band saw with ⅛" (3mm) blade, 10–14 TPI
- Oscillating drum sander with ¾" (1.9cm) drum, 180 and 240 grits
- Sanding mop with 400 grit or sandpaper for hand-sanding, 400 grit
- Small belt sander with 180- and 240-grit sanding belts
- Microfiber towels
- Clear construction adhesive (dispensed with a caulk gun) or viscous CA glue
- Acrylic clear nonyellowing exterior finish for water and UV protection

Pattern on page 97.

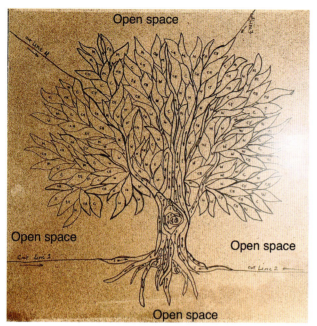

1. Lay the prepared hardboard pattern directly on top of the backer board. Your mosaic will be built on top of the backer board. The outer open spaces of the pattern will act as a guide to keep your mosaic arranged properly

2. Using a scroll saw fitted with a universal #5 blade or smaller, cut out the pattern following lines 1, 2, 3 and 4 only.

3. Reassemble the cut pattern pieces on top of the backer board. The entire pattern is now divided into four sections labeled 1, 2 3, and 4.

4. Beginning with section 1, working from left to right, cut around the root pieces all the way across the bottom of section 1. Reassemble those cut-out. open-space pieces onto the backer board.

74   Making Magnificent Wood Art

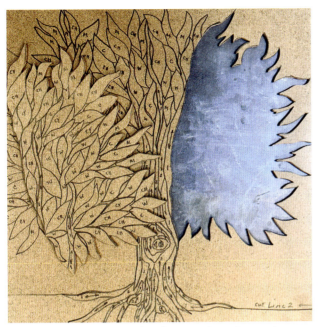

5. Cut each of the remaining four sections, just as in Step 4. Cut out the outside open space around the outer leaves and sides of the trunk *in as few pieces as possible*. Then, reassemble those pieces on the backer board.

6. Tape down the outer edge open spaces. Line the straight outer edge with tape, and then wrap the tape under the backer board. Tape any cuts you had to make between the open space pieces. These outside areas help keep the whole pattern in the correct position.

7. In section 1, cut out the trunk pieces, one pattern piece at a time, and reassemble each piece in the pattern on the backer board before moving on to the next cut. Based on my experience, this will keep everything in order. For sections 2, 3, and 4, cut the leaves, branches (branches are marked with arrows), and upper trunk out, beginning on the outer edge against the open space area and working your way to the middle of the tree. Again, cut one pattern piece at a time and place it back in the pattern before moving. Use the second intact pattern for placement reference if necessary.

Chapter 4: Projects   Carved Canopy Mosaic

8. Beginning at the roots of the tree trunk, remove the pattern piece for one of the roots and position it onto the cedar board. Position it somewhere near the bottom edge of the board with the grain running in the same direction as the arrows on the pattern piece. Trace and label the wood with the same number on the pattern piece.

9. With the scroll saw and a #7 blade, cut out this traced shape, wipe it down with a microfiber cloth, and return it to the backer board where that pattern piece used to be.

76 Making Magnificent Wood Art

10. Repeat this process for every root, trunk, and branch piece in the pattern, replacing the pattern piece with the cedar wood. As you trace the tree trunk and root pieces onto the cedar board, place them so that you use your cedar most economically with as little waste as possible. Be sure to cut on the inside of your traced line to ensure the best fit. If your cut cedar piece does not fit well into its place, observe where it needs to be trimmed and trim it on the scroll saw. Set the pattern pieces aside in case you need to recut a piece later.

Using Wood Knots in Your Mosaic

If you have a solid knot in your wood, you can position the center of the pattern knot and the surrounding circular pieces over your wood knot.

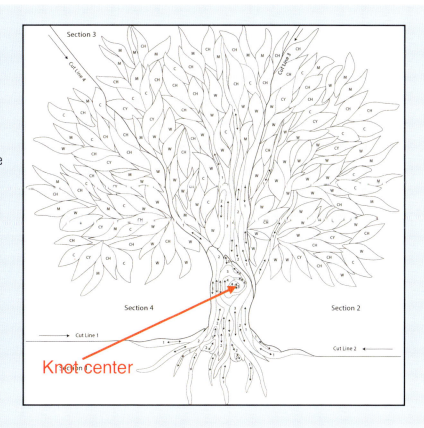

Chapter 4: Projects Carved Canopy Mosaic   **77**

11. Cut the walnut leaves. Starting in section 2, chose a pattern leaf labeled "W" and position it onto the walnut board and trace. Cut out the shape with a #7 blade on the scroll saw. Replace this walnut leaf in the mosaic and set the pattern leaf aside. Repeat for all the walnut leaves.

12. Cut the rest of the leaves. Follow the directions in the previous step for all the leaves, tracing and cutting them one at a time on their respective wood type. W=walnut, Cy=cypress, Ch=cherry, C=cedar, M=maple.

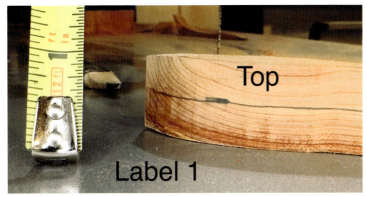
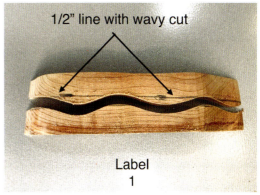

13. Locate the trunk pieces (including all roots and branches) labeled with "1." These pieces will be the lowest or most thin pieces of the tree trunk. One at a time, sculpt the trunk piece by turning it onto its side. Using a tape measure and pencil, draw a line lengthwise down the piece ½" (1.3cm) from the top. Cut along this line in a wavelike cut to remove the top ½" (1.3cm) (approximately) of surface off the piece. Discard the top part. The wavy cuts are long, loose, and shallow; not tight, deep, roller-coaster waves.

14. Sculpt each cedar trunk piece labeled 1, *one at a time.* Wipe each one down with a microfiber cloth and replace them, one by one, in the mosaic.

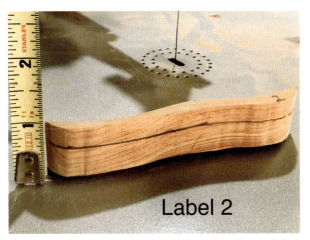
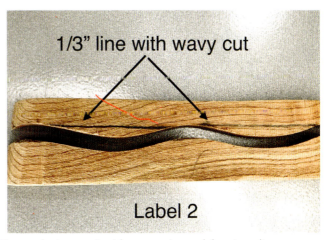

15. Sculpt the trunk pieces labeled with "2" one at a time. Turn each piece on its side, measuring and drawing a line lengthwise ⅓" (8.5mm) from the top. Cut along that line to remove the top ⅓" (8.5mm) in a wavelike cut just like the previous pieces. Discard the top and return the piece to its place in the mosaic.

Chapter 4: Projects   Carved Canopy Mosaic

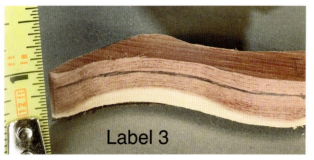

Label 3

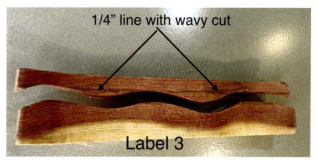

1/4" line with wavy cut

Label 3

16. Sculpt the trunk pieces labeled "3" one at a time. Turn each onto its side, draw a line lengthwise ¼" (6.4mm) from the top, and cut along that line to remove the top ¼" (6.4mm) in a wavelike cut just like the previous pieces. Return the piece to its place in the mosaic.

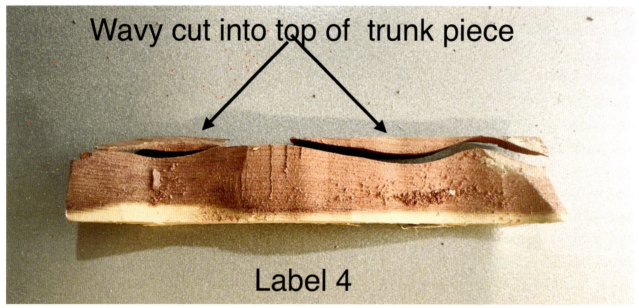

Wavy cut into top of trunk piece

Label 4

17. Finally, locate the pieces labeled "4." These pieces are the highest pieces in the trunk and are sculpted by turning them on their side and cutting a wavelike cut into the very top surface of the piece. Return each to the mosaic.

18. Here are all four of the cuts you just made. Notice that with all four cuts lined up, you can see the gradual rise in height, even though the waves obscure it slightly.

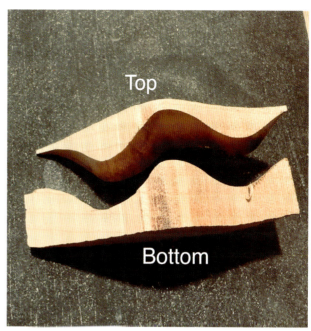

19. Sculpt the leaves. Working one at a time, remove a leaf from the mosaic. Turn the leaf on its side, hold it down firmly, and cut a deep wave into the top surface of the leaf. The wave's deepest point can be just below ½" (1.3cm) deep (approximately), and the highest point should be near the top surface. Discard the top of the leaf and replace the lower half in the mosaic after wiping it with a microfiber cloth.

20. Sand the cedar trunk, roots, and branches. Use a belt sander or oscillating drum sander fitted with 240 grit, and sand down any saw blade marks or rough areas. Heavily round the top edges for a barrel-type shape. Be careful not to take off too much material. Cedar is soft and easily sanded. Finish sand the cedar trunk pieces using a mop sander or sanding by hand with 400 grit.

21. Sand each hardwood leaf using an oscillating drum sander at 180 grit. Fit it with a ½" or 1" (13 or 25mm) drum to sand into the deep waves of the leaves. Sand down any saw blade lines or rough areas. For the cedar and cypress, sand with a 240-grit drum. Finish sand with the mop sander or sand by hand using 400-grit sandpaper.

22. Glue down the trunk pieces first. Beginning at the roots and ending at the branches, spread the viscous clear glue onto the bottom of each piece, keeping the outer edges free of glue to avoid seepage around the edges. You may need to apply a thin bead down the center of a long, thin piece. Press the piece down lightly into the backer board.

23. After you glue down the root pieces, carefully remove any open space pattern pieces against the roots before the glue fully sets so that they do not accidently get stuck to the backer board.

24. Glue down the leaves, putting a dot of glue in the center of each leaf and pressing into the backer board. Again, remove the open space pattern pieces as you go. Allow the glue to fully set before moving the mosaic.

25. Apply acrylic finish with a small paintbrush. Allow it to dry and reapply. Sand lightly with 400-grit sandpaper or mop sand. Build a frame and/or attach hanging hardware to the backer board back if desired.

Yellow Wood Mosaic

For those of you who like a challenge, this grouping of aspens is a rewarding project and a beauty to hang on your walls or give as a gift to your special person. It is more difficult than the other projects because there is more complex sculpting. However, I have worked out the best sculpting method for you, and I think you will find the steps straightforward. The name comes from a Robert Frost poem "The Road Not Taken."

If you love the mountains out west, you probably love the distinctive bark pattern on aspens that sets them apart from other trees. The horizontal lines that wrap around the tree are raised scars, evidence of its natural perpetual shedding of bark, and can look like knotty "eyes." The old timers call aspens "quakies" because the leaves attach in a unique way that causes them to tremble at the slightest breeze. I have hunted elk for their meat and hide in those remote quakies and experienced the ethereal whispers and white powdery beauty of those aspens.

For this sculpture, I used the best and most available wood for the dark knotty eyes and lines, American black walnut, but any walnut that is sufficiently dark will work. I gave the job of representing the white part of the trunks to ambrosia maple, which is mostly a stark white but also has its own scars of dark enigmatic linear shapes to create the illusion of aspen scarring and also mimic the shadows of nearby trees. The placement of the ambrosia scarring can be completely random and still work its magic. Finally, one of my favorite woods, Osage orange, was the winning choice for the yellow leaves.

Materials and Tools

- 1 square of painted backer board, 13" x 22" (33 x 55.9cm) (see page 42 for more information)
- 2 squares of 13" x 22" (33 x 55.9cm) hardboard with paper pattern glued on or pattern traced directly onto hardboards from a projector using the same method and size as the hardboard pattern (see page 44 for more information)
- Scissors
- Spray adhesive
- 8" x 24" or 4" x 48" (20.3 x 61cm or 10.2 x 121.9cm) of 1" or 1¼" (2.5 or 3.2cm) thick boards of ambrosia maple
- 4" x 12" of 1" or 1¼" (2.5 or 3.2cm) thick boards of black walnut
- 26 square inches (167.7 sq cm) of 1" (2.5cm) or thicker boards of Osage orange*
- 26 square inches (167.7 sq cm) of 1" (2.5cm) or thicker boards of padauk
- Fine-tip Sharpie or sharpened pencil
- Scroll saw with universal blades #5 and #7 or band saw with ⅛" (3mm) blade, 10–14 TPI
- Oscillating drum sander with ¾" (19mm) drum, 180 and 240 grits
- Small belt sander with 180- and 240-grit sanding belts
- Sanding mop with 400 grit or sandpaper for hand-sanding, 400 grit
- Clear construction adhesive (dispensed with a caulk gun) or viscous CA glue
- Acrylic clear nonyellowing exterior finish for water and UV protection

*If you don't have Osage orange, you can substitute yellowheart.

A Note About Wood

Both woods that make the aspen trunk, walnut and maple, need to be the same thickness. Either 1" or 1¼" (2.5 or 3.2cm).

I recommend a square inch size rather than a strict dimensional size because the leaves are very small, around 1" (2.5cm) diameter or less and because Osage orange does not come in very wide widths. Working this way gives you more freedom to purchase what is available for you. Also, you can find small lots of Osage orange on places like eBay.

Pattern on page 98.

1. Cut out the trunks. Arrange the hardboard pattern onto the backer board. Using a scroll saw fitted with a universal #5 blade or smaller, cut out each full-length trunk from the hardboard pattern. Although you see individual pieces within the trunk, try to cut the trunks in straight lines along the sides, not dipping in to follow the individual pieces. Also ignore the branches growing from the trunks and simply cut along the straight line of the trunk. The dips are a result of sanding at the final stage, so we must ignore them and follow a straight path.

2. Working one at a time, lay the cut-out trunk pattern onto the maple board. Position it so the grain lines follow the length of the trunk. Trace with a pencil or fine marker around the pattern, keeping the tip of your pencil tight against the pattern. Remove the pattern and label the top surface of each outlined trunk on the maple board with a T and the back of each trunk, on the backside of the board, with a B.

3. With the scroll saw fitted with a universal #7 blade, cut the traced trunk lines on the maple wood. Place the maple wood trunks into the pattern.

4. Mark the aspen trunks. The goal is to sculpt each trunk into a half-barrel shape with the scroll saw. At the top end and bottom end of each trunk draw a half-barrel shape to use as a reference.

86   Making Magnificent Wood Art

5. Shape the middle trunk. Where the middle aspen trunk intersects the right aspen trunk, some of its trunk narrows to a point, so you cannot draw a half-barrel shape on this end. Instead, sculpt this lower area as a half barrel that decreases in size.

6. To sculpt away the materials, cut away starting at the top corners of the maple trunks and ending at the bottom corners in thin strips. You will need to hold the tree trunk on one edge in front of the band saw or scroll saw blade to begin to cut away at each top edge.

This sculpting step requires you to hold the wood on edge on the scroll saw platform. One way to help navigate this is to hold the trunk firmly down on both ends and guide it through the blade. If you find that the wood is jumping, the blade is probably grabbing. Try a smaller size blade, and cut slower through the wood.

7. Cut the entire length of the maple trunk with each cut, keeping the depth even until you have cut your half-barrel shape. This will take multiple cuts. When you are first learning this technique, cut thin strips off at a time so that your do not accidently cut off too much with a wayward blade. With practice, you can make this cut in three or four strips.

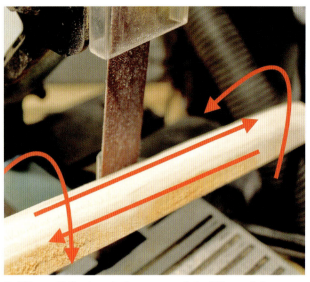

8. When all the trunks have a crude half-barrel shape, begin to sand them on a belt sander with 180 grit to remove any remaining wood material and smooth them. It helps to rotate around the half-barrel shape as you slide back and forth, down the length of the trunk from one end to the middle. Then, flip the trunk over and sand the other end the same way. Sand down any high or uneven ridges and clean off any dust with a microfiber towel.

9. Using the *paper* Yellow Wood Mosaic pattern, cut out the full-length trunks with scissors, following along the outside straight edges, but this time *include* any branches that extend from the trunk. (I traced the pattern onto builder's paper, but it is too stiff. I recommend a softer paper.)

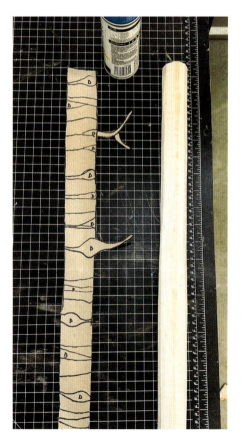

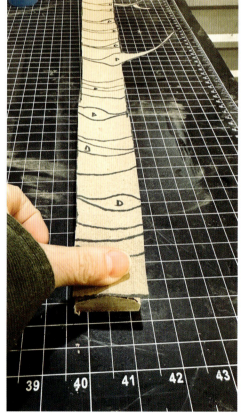

10. Remove the maple trunks from the backer board and set them onto your workspace. Using spray adhesive, lightly spray the back of one of the cut-out paper aspen trunks, covering it completely. Position the top and bottom centers of the paper pattern on the top and bottom centers of the matching maple trunk and press the pattern onto the trunk. Repeat for the remaining two trunks. (I had to tape the edges of my pattern because of the stiff paper.)

Making Magnificent Wood Art

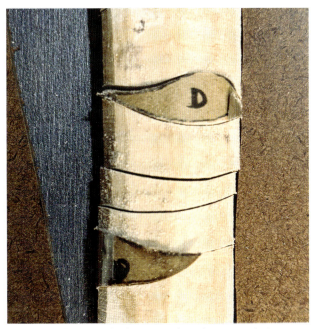

11. Using the scroll saw and a #7 blade, one at a time, cut out the individual trunk pieces. Replace them into their positions in the pattern on the backer board. Remove the adhered pattern from all trunk pieces without the label D. Leave the paper pattern attached to those with the label D.

12. Remove the bottommost trunk piece labeled D. Remove the paper pattern adhered to it and discard it. Take that maple piece and trace it onto your walnut board. We are not following the wood grain with these pieces, so position them in any direction to save space on your walnut board.

13. Using a scroll saw and a #7 blade, cut along the traced lines and place that walnut piece back into its spot in the aspen trunk. Discard the maple template of that piece. Repeat for all D pieces except those with extended branch pieces.

Chapter 4: Projects **Yellow Wood Mosaic**

14. For the D extended branch pieces, carefully remove the sticky paper pattern from the maple template and position this paper pattern piece onto the walnut board. If necessary, respray the back of the pattern. Trace and cut the pieces, or skip the tracing and cut around the paper pattern. Replace this walnut trunk piece back into the aspen trunk. Discard the original maple template of this piece.

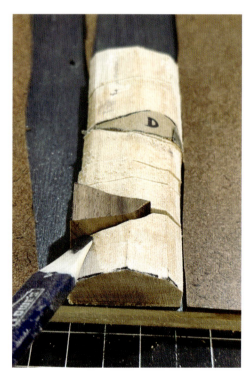

15. Sculpt the walnut trunk piece to match the barrel shape of the maple pieces. Without removing any of the trunk pieces, trace the barrel shape of the adjoining maple trunk piece onto the walnut piece.

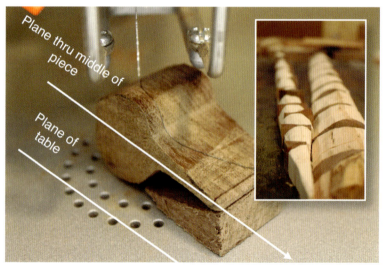

16. Remove the walnut trunk piece and turn it on its side, so the tracing is face up. If one side is significantly thinner than the other side, prop up the shallow end with a piece of scrap wood so that an imaginary line running through the midline of the walnut piece is parallel to the scroll saw table. You can tape the scrap wood to the walnut trunk piece if you cannot keep it in place as you cut. Cut the traced line with the scroll saw (you will also be cutting through the scrap wood with this cut). Replace the walnut trunk piece in the pattern.

Making Magnificent Wood Art

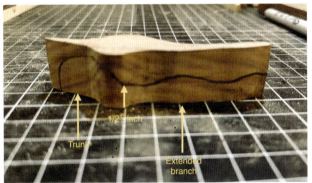

17. For the walnut trunk pieces that extend into branches, trace the rounded part of the trunk until you reach approximately a ½" (1.3cm) from the bottom on the branch side of the trunk piece. At this half-inch point, begin to extend your line in a wavy fashion to the end of the branch.

18. Sculpt this extended trunk piece by turning it onto its side and cutting the traced line. Replace the walnut piece into the pattern (the hardboard underneath this extended branch can be removed in the next step).

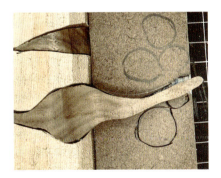

19. Cut out the leaves and branches of the hardboard pattern. Then, replace them in the pattern. Also replace the hardboard occupying the big open spaces as placeholders for the overall pattern arrangement. Alternatively, to help with the leaf and branch positioning, mark a dot on the backer board under the center of each leaf with a marker. Mark one dot under each end of the branches, and replace the pieces. This way, when you need to return the leaf or branch to its position, you can easily find where it goes.

Chapter 4: Projects Yellow Wood Mosaic

20. Starting with the pattern branches labeled D, trace, cut and sculpt them *one at a time*. Position a branch onto the walnut board and trace it. Then, cut out the traced shape with the scroll saw. Sculpt the walnut branch by turning it on its side lengthwise, and cut off the top ½" (1.3cm), approximately, in a wavelike pattern. Discard the cut-away top and replace the bottom in the pattern. Discard the branch hardboard pattern as well.

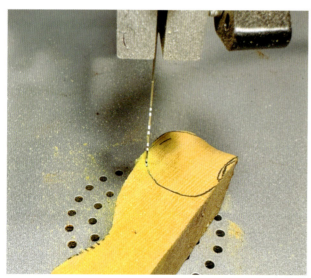

21. For the leaves, trace, cut, and sculpt them *one at a time*. Leaf hardboard patterns labeled Y (yellow) are traced onto the Osage orange boards, and those labeled O (orange) are traced onto padauk boards. Working one at a time, remove one hardboard leaf pattern and position it onto the appropriate wood board, trace, and cut out the shape with the scroll saw.

22. Next, sculpt the leaf by turning it on its side and cutting it in half lengthwise in a wavelike pattern. Since many of the leaves are very small, you will not be able to create much of a wave, and that is ok. Hold the leaf down firmly as you make the cut because it may cause the blade to grab and the wood to jump. Be extra careful here, as your fingers are very close to the blade. Discard the top half of the wood leaf and replace the bottom half back into the pattern. Discard the hardboard leaf pattern.

23. To sand down the trunk pieces, use a belt sander or oscillating drum sander fitted with a 240-grit drum. Your maple pieces are already somewhat sanded, which is why we're starting with a 240 grit. If you discover this is too fine, begin with a 180 grit. Starting at the bottom of each maple trunk, sand the top of each trunk piece until it is smooth. Correct any uneven areas. Round the inside edges slightly where the trunk pieces meet one another to fit together.

24. Repeat the sanding process with the next piece above it. Sand it to match the shape of the previously sanded trunk piece, and continue moving up the trunk. One exception is the trunk that tapers at the bottom, giving it the illusion of disappearing behind the other trunk. Sand this trunk, beginning at the bottom and increasing gradually in size so that the end of each piece matches the adjoining piece. Finish sand with a mop sander or hand-sand with up to 400 grit.

25. Sand the branches with a belt sander or drum sander beginning with 180- or 240-grit sandpaper if the walnut is already quite smooth. Sand the sides and top surface to smooth. Round the long edges of the top surface. Be careful not to take off too much material since they are so thin. Finish with mop sander or hand sanding at 240 and then 400 grit.

26. Sand the leaves with the oscillating drum sander fitted with 180-grit sandpaper. Sand down any cut lines or rough spots on top and sides. Round out the sharp outside edge slightly. Finish sanding with the mop sander or hand sanding at 240 and 400 grit.

Chapter 4: Projects   Yellow Wood Mosaic

27. After sanding, apply acrylic clear nonyellowing exterior finish to the top and sides of every piece for color retention and moisture control. Allow it to dry. Reapply. Optionally, sand again with the mop sander at 400 grit because the finish raises the grain and roughens the surface.

28. Glue the trunks to the backer board first. Beginning at the bottom of each trunk, spread a viscous glue onto the bottom of each trunk piece, staying at least ¼" (6.4mm) away from the outer edges to avoid seepage around the edge.

29. Apply glue at the end that meets the next trunk piece, staying away from the top edge. Take your time to line up the trunk pieces as you go so that the sides are all aligned and there are no offset trunk pieces. If you left the hardboard pattern in the open spaces, remove it from the backer board now in case any glue has spread to under the hardboard, as you do not want to accidentally glue this to your backer board. Be careful not to move the trunks, branches, or leaves.

30. Glue down the branches, following the same recommendations for the trunk. Finally, glue down the leaves, putting a dot of glue in the center of each leaf and pressing into the backer board. Allow the glue to fully set before moving the mosaic. Build a frame and/or attach hanging hardware to the back of the backer board if desired.

Patterns

Photocopy and enlarge the patterns by the percentage indicated. See more about resizing on page 43. You can also download the full-size template files by following the QR code or going to the website: foxpatterns.com/making-magnificent-wood-art/

Floral Mandala Mosaic
Photocopy at 225%

Rose Reverie Mosaic
Photocopy at 150%

GRAIN DIRECTION

96   Making Magnificent Wood Art

Carved Canopy Mosaic
Photocopy at 300%

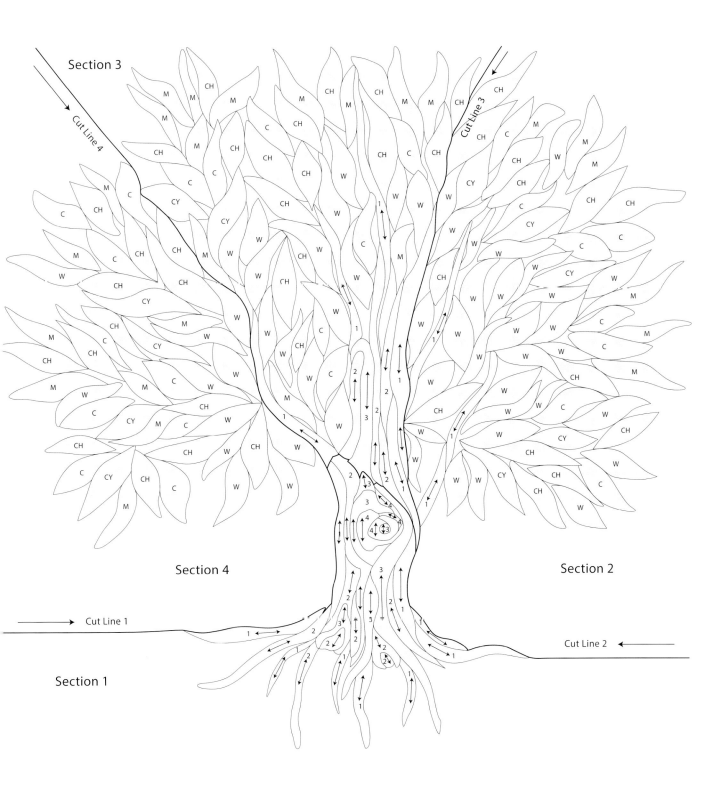

Chapter 4: Projects Patterns **97**

Yellow Wood Mosaic

Photocopy at 250%

Aspens, 2022. Walnut, padauk, pink ivory. 36" x 48" (91.4 x 121.9cm).

Chapter 5: Journey of a Wood Artist

The Balinese have a saying, "We have no art. We just do everything as beautifully as we can." To me, this means that whether you are sitting at a computer writing code or digging a ditch, the way you do it *matters*. Creativity is really a birthright. When I was a little girl, I remember how utterly fluid my creativity was. If I put on a blanket, it immediately became a cape, and I was a superhero. I fully played my part in this very real fantasy, and there was no "jolt to reality" when it was over. As every one of you knows, you simply shifted your attention to the next reality. All of it was real. When I make art, it serves so well to release that agile creativity once again. It's kind of like the saying, "Would you rather be right or happy?" To suspend being right or "knowing" for a place of not knowing and exploring all the options is its own kind of nirvana for me.

I love the rawness of this aspen piece. I left the leaves pretty rough, and now I am impressed with how bold I was back then. You can see how many times I cut the trunks to create lines and shadows, and the result is beautiful.

Chapter 5: Journey of a Wood Artist

Probably taken around 1978; my mom was taking the photo, so she wasn't included in this shot; however her effect on my ideas about life, vitality, health, and creativity was enormous and still is. She is currently 80 years old and can run circles around most 30 year olds, both mentally and physically. She continues to show me what is possible.

I recall being around seven when my parents, who had no formal college education or art training of any kind, were studying Rembrandt and teaching themselves his oil painting techniques. I would peek into the room and be immediately hit with the unfamiliar smells of turpentine and paint. I'd glimpse at them deep in concentration with brushes in hand. Then I tiptoed away, filled with wonder to see my parents in the *very act of making art*. I see those paintings every time I visit my parents' house, and while they are nicely done, that was not the point. They had a desire to paint, did it to the best of their ability, and then stopped when their interest dried up. My seven-year-old eyes took all of this in, and it would later serve me.

A year or two later, my life took an unusual and unsettling turn. We moved into a children's "home." Here, orphaned or destitute children and teenagers lived, and volunteer surrogate parents would live in the houses to take care of them. My parents were some of the surrogates, and my siblings and I became part of this odd household. Going from a safe, stable family environment to a house of 12 kids that desperately needed parents to love them and give them attention could have been very disorienting, and it was, at times. But I knew that, like the Rembrandt paintings, this was just another foray into a creative adventure. I was only eight years old, but I had begun, without too much understanding, to feel a pattern and to know that we would be moving on to the next thing soon.

At this point, I did not have any outstanding creative talent that presented itself, but notably my mom wrote down that I was unusually dexterous and "quick with my hands." Under the surface, a burgeoning aptitude to follow my own unique path and pursuits was being developed. I was being shaped by eccentric parents, only a smattering of schooling, and an unconventional life more than I realized at the time.

I remember going to school in the fourth grade when my family had just moved to remote Arkansas on top of a mountain in the Ozarks. For me, it was just another move. I was supremely oblivious that my parents were worried about the political climate and wanted to be self-sufficient in case the economy went south. Many times, I bathed in an outdoor tub with spring water that was heated by lighting a fire under it. We heated the house solely with a wood stove in the living room. When I was nine years old, my sister and I milked a cow and took care of the animals early every morning before anyone was awake. I specifically remember one early morning before school when the water in the pond froze. The animals needed water to drink. My sister and I were not strong enough to break the thick ice on the pond with an ax. We eventually found a big rock and lifting it together, we dropped it on the pond surface edge until it broke through. It did not occur to me to ask my dad for help. I knew he expected me and my sister to figure it out and having been given confidence, I did.

The oldest four kids with bass caught from the pond. More than likely, it was our dinner for the night. This photo also shows my adorable adopted Korean sister, at this point in the US for only four years. My baby brother is not pictured.

My oldest sister and I, right after milking the cow.

I did not attend much high school. I did go to 10th grade and the first half of 11th grade. During that time, I took several math classes and had an incredible art teacher, Ms. Black-Libby, who nurtured the flickering artistic flame burning in me. She introduced me to all kinds of art, and it started to dawn on me that I liked working with materials that I could manipulate with my hands, such as clay, printmaking, and batik. Despite this, I could not shake the feeling that I was wasting my time in high school. On the day I withdrew from school to get my GED, the school officials one by one sent me into their offices, warning me against the mistake I was making. They probably meant well, but it really shook

Chapter 5: Journey of a Wood Artist   **101**

me—not because they disagreed with my decision but because facing their disproving authority on my own at sixteen was hard. It was my first experience of standing up to authorities to follow my path, and it got a lot easier after that.

I took the GED and started college, majoring in chemistry. I went further and received a master's degree in biochemistry. My life plan at the time was to work in the sciences, but that did not happen. First of all, I was not a good scientist. Many of the things that make my current artwork distinctive were the very qualities that made me a terrible experimental scientist. In a science experiment, you cannot take interesting detours mid-experiment, or use a shortcut method that might work, or inventively tinker with anything. I was really good at thinking about DNA repair and designing experiments. However, I found that the precise measuring and repetition, which are absolutely required for a reliable experiment, were making me miserable. After two and a half years had passed, I had great difficulty getting myself to repeat an experiment and was losing interest because of it. Instead of getting easier with experience and time, my resistance to this type of repetition was getting stronger. My reaction was to hide what I thought was a character flaw and make excuses to myself about why I was so disengaged, instead of examining and accepting it as a part of me that deserved to be there and had a purpose. After two and a half years, I finally had enough, wrapped up my experiments, and defended my masters thesis at the University of North Carolina at Chapel Hill. It wasn't a PhD like I had intended, but I was free. Plus,

This shows my early experimentation with floor tile mosaics with reclaimed tile.

Making Magnificent Wood Art

I was pregnant with my second child, which was the best reason to cut the process short.

It was not until I was raising my four children, about five years later, that I began to really feel the call of my creativity. Something that had been in me from the beginning was maturing, and even though it was an incredibly busy time of my life and my kids took utmost priority, I began to experiment with painting. Canvases did not really suit me; I didn't like being bound by those four straight sides. It felt claustrophobic, so I painted scenes on walls and furniture. Two years later, my husband at the time and I built a house. We did as much of the work as possible by ourselves. I fully dove into designing large tile mosaics throughout the main floor and especially on kitchen backsplashes and countertops. I remember many days where I designed the mosaics by day, and when my husband came home in the afternoon to be with the kids, I would escape to the new house and spend the evening and into the night laying tile. Time did not exist while I was engaged in this process. Energy surged through me even after an exhausting day. As long as I had a mosaic tile project, I felt possessed and almost feverish to finish it.

My first tile project, where I had the idea to use wood for the trunks of these stylized trees to create a built-in cutting board on these kitchen countertops.

It was becoming obvious to me that I possessed an instinctive drive to make things. With more examination, I noticed my fervor and delight to put pieces of different materials together in unexpected ways that were beautiful but unique. Whatever objects or materials I had in front of me, I needed to see them outside what they conventionally were. For example, my great-uncle-in-law gave me some old scythe handles—long, curved, cylindrical handles from when people cut down wheat or weeds by hand in wide, sweeping arm motions. I think they were made of oak. My mind's eye immediately discarded any beliefs I had about what the scythe handle actually was, so that I could play the game of seeing the object as if for the first time, asking what it could become. I cut these handles lengthwise, right down the middle, on a table saw, mounted them horizontally above my kitchen sink, and created a tiled mosaic under these curved wood shapes. That was the first time I had ever

Chapter 5: Journey of a Wood Artist

incorporated wood into a mosaic. We are always presented clues along the way about our unique purpose, and often these clues are pervasive behaviors that are right under our very noses.

Here, I need to go back to that mountain in Arkansas when I was nine. One aspect of my life that came to a head at this point in the story started back then. My parents became part of a very exclusive religious sect while we lived in Arkansas. As a quick background, the sect was highly seclusive, controlling, and encouraged its members to only make friends among themselves. It was organized into groups that met in homes for religious ceremonies weekly and had very strict ideas about how to think, how to speak, and how to live in the world. They also assigned high value to men and what they had to say but assigned very little value to women.

Life happens, and change is inevitable, but growth is a choice. The container of a marriage within the religious sect and the container of religion became like the four sides of the canvas. I became claustrophobic and suffocated. Deciding to leave was like ripping off the dirty bandage of a deep wound so it could heal. I closed my eyes tight and did it. The heads of the sect called a meeting with me and my husband, and I found myself, again, calling forth an inner grit to stand up to the current authority. Leaving meant not only leaving a husband and the religion but also leaving parents, siblings, and all the friends in the sect—the only people I had in the world at the time. I felt like a zebra who had been raised in a zoo. I was told that this zoo was my true home, but now I escaped to the great wild and had a lot to learn. An outside-the-sect cousin came to my aid and basically, with great insight, took me through a deconditioning program that I am forever grateful for. My education came to my rescue, and I began to teach at a local university. Art felt like a luxury, and creating a safe haven for me and my kids was paramount.

My very first wood mosaic art piece. The arms stretching over the head felt like freedom and the audacity to be vulnerable.

Photo Credit: Mia Phillips

Working in a borrowed shop, I built all the female forms with a rickety bandsaw and a small belt sander.

Fast forward to my mid-forties—after raising pigs, co-owning a music venue and bar, riding a motorcycle through Alaska and the Yukon, ending a long-term relationship, working as a chef for two years on a private yacht, designing commercial spaces, training for three intense years in Latin dance—my life had begun to feel like the mosaics I had made, a multitude of crazy experiences now cohesively and harmoniously existing as a single mosaic. I felt a peace about myself I never had before.

One day, after a week of riding a bicycle through mountain passes in Colorado, near the end of my long-term relationship, I walked into the house of a friend and saw an unusual painting of a woman with her arms stretched above her head. The paint was applied in singular thick streaks, like a mosaic painting. After returning home, I could not forget that painting and the expression of pure freedom coming from this painted woman. I finally decided to create my version of it, but not in tile. I decided to create it in wood because I needed organic curves. It became my very first art piece in the early days of this style of wood mosaic.

After this art piece was born, more pieces poured out of me. Mostly, they were wood mosaics of women in ferocious battle poses or strong poses—suggesting being beaten down but now rising up. These wood mosaics literally

This early work of a female form was cut from an old heart pine board. The patterning gaps are what gives her body most of its texture.

This is one of my human form pieces. Even though this piece came before I developed my sculpting technique, it speaks volumes to me of strength—facing life with sword in hand—while also being beautiful and feminine. The Skirt and the Sword. I made and designed the mask from copper, which allowed me to avoid a face (not within my skillset at the time), but more importantly, it kept her anonymous. She could be anyone. I showed this piece for barely two days before a woman called me and asked if she could Venmo me and take it from the wall that day.

Chapter 5: Journey of a Wood Artist

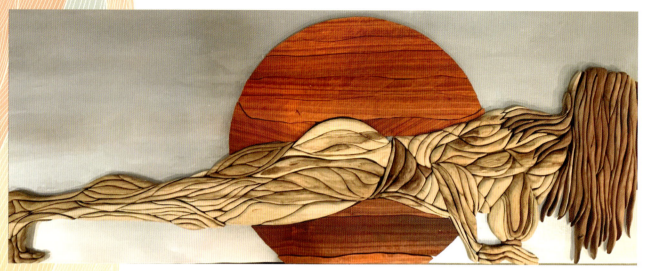

This mosaic was originally flat and unsculpted from my early days. I was experimenting with patterning but not sculpting yet. I added the setting sun later and sculpted the pieces to have some shape. I envisioned this woman as having been knocked down, but she is now able to rise up. The sun is setting, but it is not too late.

More early public art pieces. My client was opening a cool industrial brewery and taproom (Mordecai Beverage in Raleigh, NC) and wanted to bring some of the outside in. He had the idea of "tap roots" leading to the beer taps.

gushed out of me, and I felt completely compelled to make them. All I owned at the time was a jigsaw, which I taught myself to use, and a sander, but that felt like magic. Each mosaic became increasingly more intricate in the patterning as I grew in my technique. The surfaces of the mosaics were still flat since I had not yet developed sculpting. I began to use the woodshop of an old friend and was introduced to a scroll saw and a band saw. The sky became the limit as far as I was concerned, and I set about finding the capabilities of these two saws.

I began to post my progress on social media and to show some works at the local coffee shop. It's funny to remember how bold I was with showing those early mosaics, even though they were so flawed, but I could not have been prouder or more focused to get better. Lovely people noticed my art and felt their own particular emotions toward it. I felt and

Photo Credit: Red Feather West

A beautiful blended family of seven commissioned me to create seven unique trees that represented each of the family members. I created these trees so that the roots of each touched the trees beside it.

feel that the amount of passion and energy I put into my work is directly proportional to the amount of emotion someone feels when viewing it. My pieces began to sell for hundreds of dollars, even some reaching the thousands. My confidence began to grow that I could do this art in a sustainable way. Meanwhile, I supported myself with bartending and personal cheffing for busy working families. In my living situation at the time, I was caretaker for a beautiful, old Arts and Crafts house in exchange for living there, so I was able to create a lot of art in a very short period. Commissions started to come in, and I accepted whatever opportunity came my way.

This is an early public work of art in Raleigh, NC, which is a flat mosaic before I learned how to sculpt. This is still the largest piece of art I have ever made (about 20' x 16' [6.1 x 4.9m] or so). I did not know how I was going to do it, but when the opportunity came, I said yes and would figure it out later. It took six strong men, me, and a lift to hang these pieces that were hundreds of pounds. Thanks guys.

My first public works commission came pretty early on, and I agreed to make three huge trees to be mounted on the front of a building in Raleigh, North Carolina. I had no idea how I was going to do it, but I said yes, and then figured it out later. Thankfully, I had the help of the love of my life, my then-boyfriend and now-husband, who graciously repairs all my equipment and makes my frames (measuring is still difficult for me!).

Photo Credit: Simon Griffiths Photography

Chapter 5: Journey of a Wood Artist

Bo is a soulful, calm horse, so I kept the movement in the pieces at a minimum and gave special attention to his eyes for expression. I layered the mane wood over the neck wood, so pieces of the neck could show between mane strands.

Bo, 2020. Walnut, mahogany, sycamore, maple. Commission from Truckee, CA. 48" x 48" (121.9 x 121.9cm).

Piercing eyes through the wintery landscape, this wolf looks right through you. I sculpted each piece of the fur with a random wave into the top surface to create the illusion of tufts of fur. The snout is made of the thickest wood, so it projects into the 3D plane the highest.

Wolf, 2020. Walnut and sycamore. 33" x 37" (83.8 x 94cm).

Chapter 5: Journey of a Wood Artist **109**

Playa Dominicana, 2021. Walnut, cherry, poplar. 25" x 38" (63.5 x 96.5cm).

This tree is similar to the aspen in technique. Variable segmented cuts up the trunk end in a cluster of raw wood scraps to form the palm crown.

Shimmer Mountains, 2021. Soft maple, American black walnut, padauk, Osage orange. 38" x 30" (96.5 x 76.2cm).

This was my second aspen mosaic. By this time, I had figured out how to best create the trunks. The wormy maple gives the trunks some scars and realistic discoloration.

Tsunami, 2021. Walnut and maple. 40" x 28" (101.6 x 71.1cm).

The photograph does not do this one justice. Viewed in person, it has fantastic depth, texture, and motion. I patterned this wave from several photographs, observing how the wave gave off spray at the top and curled. I could have done so much more with this, but sometimes you have to be finished and not gild the lily. I used walnut for the deep shadows between ripples. Ultimately, my inspiration came from the famous Japanese woodblock print, *The Great Wave*.

After that commission, I fell into a time of great dissatisfaction with my art. It was missing something, and I couldn't understand what that something was. Back in the woodshop, I created and threw away for weeks, probably months. What emerged from that period, of what I would call a melancholy, was a technique that sculpted the entire top surface of the mosaic. This technique was still in development, and frankly, will always remain in development, but it allowed me to put so much more expression into my artwork that I previously craved to capture. The low point magically lifted. Soon, I was back to making commissioned works and putting my work in galleries, breweries, and coffee shops.

The trunk on this piece is very thick and chunky, giving it a real tactile feeling. I patterned the trunk by following some grain variations on the gum wood, which I think worked out well.

Carved Sunlight, 2022. Gum wood, maple, walnut, ash, cherry, mahogany. 30" x 38" (76.2 x 96.5cm).

I patterned the tree so that the branches nearly touch the ground. Large leaves are cut down the center to indicate the vein in the leaf.

Magnolia, 2022. Gum, walnut, mahogany, cherry, cedar, ash. 45" x 45" (114.3 x 114.3cm).

Instead of creating separate leaves on this willow's weeping branches, I cut wavy curves down a straight piece of wood, curving them over at the top. The waves give the illusion of viewing the leaves from a distance.

Weeping Cascade, 2022. Walnut, maple, mahogany. 36" x 34" (91.4 x 86.4cm).

Chapter 5: Journey of a Wood Artist

Mandala Maze, 2022. Padauk, Osage orange, poplar, walnut, cedar, maple, gum, ash. 40" x 20" (101.6 x 50.8cm).

This work is obviously very similar to the mandala project in this book. I made the individual pieces a bit longer and more flowy to look like flowers. A couple of them are falling out of the frame which feels very organic, like they were captured in a photo.

I used the same sculpting technique on the body as I did on the fur on the wolf, which makes the feathers look as if they are overlapping.

Polish Crest, 2022. Commission. Walnut, sycamore, cherry, mahogany, Osage orange, padauk, and a piece of the client's Polish grandfather's wooden hammer handle. 36" x 24" (91.4 x 61cm).

Purple Shade, 2022. Gum, walnut, mahogany, cherry, maple, cedar. 26" x 22" (66 x 55.9cm).

I used quite thin wood for this one, and it appears beautifully delicate. The leaves are mostly similar tones with a contrasting trunk that works very well.

Sway, 2022. Maple, walnut, mahogany, ash, gum, sycamore, cherry, cedar. 36" x 38" (91.4 x 96.5cm).

This tree is one of my favorites and is my second swaying tree in a series of five. Curving the trunk gives this piece a sense of movement and shifts the composition from the center. The great variety in the shapes of the leaves also creates a sense of wind blowing through the canopy.

Chapter 5: Journey of a Wood Artist

Sunny-Side Up, 2023.
Gum, cedar, walnut
maple, cherry, ash.
28" x 20" (71.1 x 50.8cm).

I love how alive this little tree feels. The leaves are curvy and long, contributing to the sense of movement. The sun is shining in the top right corner so all the outside leaves on the right are white maple, gradually darkening toward the left side.

This is an example of zooming out to give your subject a context or a story. This allowed me to add some cattails to help suggest a body of water, along with the blue in the painting.

Heron, 2023. Cedar, maple, walnut, cherry, Osage orange. 25" x 40" (63.5 x 101.6cm).

Resonance, 2023. Ebony, cedar, mahogany, walnut. 34" x 28" (86.4 x 71.1cm).

My client wanted a mosaic for her music room, while also having a botanical theme. I patterned the interior of the ebony note as leaves to soften this rigid notation. Curving "vines" of walnut create the illusion of weaving around the musical note.

Deep Waters, 2024. Walnut, zebrawood, wormy maple. 50" x 30" (127 x 76.2cm).

A magnificent beast floats buoyantly just below the surface. You can see how I used much thicker wood for the big fin, since it projects into the foreground the most. Ripples through the wood of the body mimic viewing it through the watery depths.

This is a true example of creating patterning that suggests the real-life version. I made the large flipper's surface smooth but very segmented into a "scale" pattern. The coral floats in an underwater dance.

Under the Sea, 2023. Mahogany, gum, walnut, cedar. 22" x 28" (55.9 x 71.1cm).

Chapter 5: Journey of a Wood Artist

Whispers of Dawn, 2023. Walnut, maple, heart pine, padauk, Osage orange. 40" x 28" (101.6 x 71.1cm).

This is an example of a zoomed-out perspective. It allows there to be more objects in the mosaic, but each object is limited in its detail because the pieces would be too small. For this mosaic, I needed to portray the silence and stillness of a forest.

Year of the Wood Dragon, 2023. Zebrawood, maple, gum, cherry, ebony, cedar, Osage orange. 48" x 48" (121.9 x 121.9cm).

This is an example of using a heavily striped grain to an advantage. I used the grain to follow the direction of the bat-like wings from the spine of the wing to the bottom tip. This is actually more difficult than it might seem, and I threw out many sections of wing to get it right.

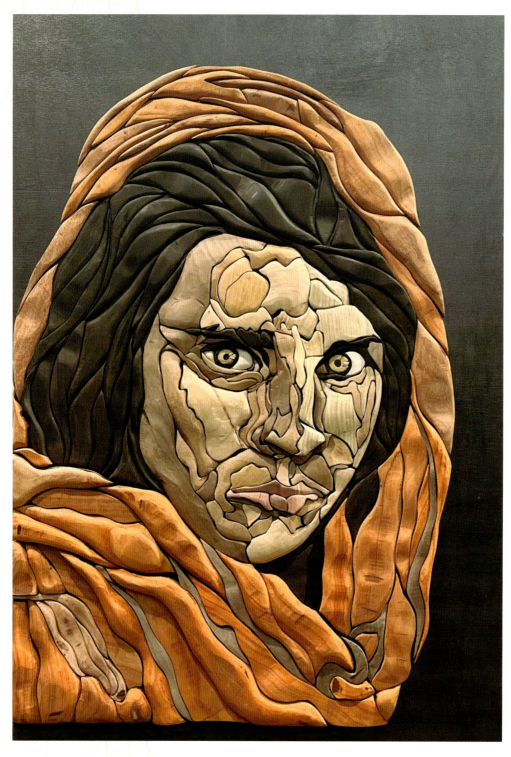

Afghan Girl, 2024. Padauk, cedar, ebony, walnut, pink ivory, mahogany, maple, gum, Osage orange. 28" x 38" (71.1 x 96.5cm).

This personal favorite piece presented quite a challenge. I used angular pieces for the face to give a look of quiet strength. I was also careful with the patterning of the eyes and wood choices to get that intense look. There is a nice contrast to the softer flow of the garment.

Fairy Forest, 2024. Walnut, cedar, maple, cherry, poplar. 48" x 40" (121.9 x 101.6cm).

I made this ethereal tree using some wood off my clients' property. They gave me carte blanche on the style, and this fairylike tree emerged. Notice that the leaves are layered onto the branches and each other. Moreover, they are very thick and wavy because both sides are sculpted. Instead of having a flat bottom, they are more like a real leaf.

Heron at the Lakehouse, 2024. Walnut, cherry, cedar, maple, ash, padauk, ebony. 33" x 28" (83.8 x 71.1cm).

For this piece, I think I used 2½" (6.4cm) wood for the thickest feathers. It's a chunky piece with a huge tactile presence. Perfect for a lakehouse.

The patterning in this piece is very individual. It could have been patterned 100 different ways. The swirly patterning of the face highlights her cheekbones and forehead and gives her a feminine quality, while the bold and prominent ebony eyebrows and eyes tell a different story. I had difficulty with the neck and finally settled on this pattern. Most of my wood and patterning decisions were made to best portray her personality.

In Flight, 2024. Cherry, ash, maple, cedar, mahogany, walnut, padauk, ebony. 26" x 38" (66 x 96.5cm).

There is lots and lots of movement in this piece due to wavy sculpting cuts in each feather that do not align with the next feather. Small pieces that curl out and away on the body also indicate small feathers and movement.